VIETNAM WAR RECALL

VIETNAM WAR RECALL

The Best and the Worst Days of My Life

MICHAEL J. CONTOS

ISBN: 978-0-578-93823-3

CONTENTS

Dedicated to Victor Lee Ellinger,
First lieutenant and platoon leader of
Charlie Company, Second Battalion, Twenty-Fifth Army Infantry Division

PREFACE

Two persons helped me revisit the Vietnam War without having to dodge bullets, escape booby traps, or pick leeches that clung to your bare skin like the demons that beseech the saints before their beatification. Each came into my life at different times. One was a medical doctor who allowed me to simply be with my memories, many of which may have been reconstructed while I looked back at a time when I was barely out of my teenage years and leading a combat infantry platoon at age twenty-one. The second holy man served as a machine gunner on a helicopter crew during the Vietnam War.

I call both of these men my mentors: enlightened beings who helped me see myself without the discolored lenses of my youth or the glasses I used in adulthood to rationalize most, if not all, of my life events.

One would end up serving the Dalai Lama as a physician, while the other, a Vietnam veteran himself, would be trained at Thich Nhat Hahn's Plum Village in France before seeking ordination as a priest in a Zen Buddhist tradition of Japan. I am as indebted to the one as I am to the other, for without their presence, I would not have gained the courage to look within at what I call the worst day of my life. Through the use of meditative techniques, I have embraced that tumultuous day and been able to remove all labels I had attached to it. I saw, for the first time, neither the good nor the bad of a friendly fire explosion but a travesty of war void of any meaning except the one I conjured up in my own mind. I saw this event through guilt, shame, and remorse for forty years without a reprieve or time off for good behavior.

▲   ▲   ▲

I wrote and wrote for five straight days while at a meditation retreat with Barry Kerzin, a Tibetan Buddhist monk who introduced me to a method of compassion whereby you absorb, or take on in your mind, the pain and suffering of others while bestowing loving-kindness to them in return. Start with a loved one, then someone neutral, and lastly try it with an enemy, he advised. It gets tougher the more you try it but easier when you feel the barriers of anger, rage, and hatred start to dissipate and you treat each friend, enemy, and neutral person the same.

It's called equanimity.

Claude "AnShin" Thomas, another monk, focused on the breathing wherever and whenever I'd come into his presence. I learned to breathe and meditate while sitting on a cushion in the traditional meditative pose, as well as when walking in a line with other meditators focusing our awareness on everything and nothing at the same time. We next turned to eating meditation, where we learned to chew each bite at least fifty times each. Yes, fifty times each is no typo! Try chewing mashed potatoes this way, folks. It can't be done by a novice, but I heard that if you reach a really high level of consciousness…well, I never made it beyond ten or fifteen chews, so I never found out.

Let's not forget the remaining method of meditation, perhaps the one where all forms of meditation are gearing us to eventually dwell: in our daily lives off the mat and in all our waking moments. This is "working" meditation, and it can be done at any time of the day or night, minute by minute, second by second. All you need to do is to focus on the present moment, to discipline your mind to be aware of the single breath you are now experiencing, and to let all thoughts dissipate. You can drive a car, read a book, or watch television while meditating as long as your awareness is on the present.

Sound easy?

No way, Jose!

I wrote my story longhand in May and transcribed and edited it the following April, seeing so many more things manifest in this process. Memories long suppressed from the war began to emerge. They scared me. While writing about how fearful I was that a sniper would shoot and kill a member of the squad I had been leading, it dawned on me that the sniper was not shooting at any of my men. That son of a bitch was shooting at me, the first lieutenant, who was leading the grunts. I faced this possibility and couldn't help but wonder why I was not killed like another junior officer, who was killed in action by an enemy sniper.

The attempt by the sniper to kill me still haunts me. And that became a main reason why I wanted to share my story with others. The more veterans speak out against war, the more reasonable persons will pay heed and listen to the voices of experience. War is never the answer unless you're Michael the Archangel and you're fighting a guy named Lucifer who refuses to acknowledge the divine providence above us all. "To hell with him" is what any veteran will tell you and be the first ones to sign up for a campaign against such a son of a bitch, if I can use that term without quite knowing anything about Lucifer's maternal connection, if he ever had one.

Included in this saga are articles I wrote while meditating about the war and the posttraumatic stress disorder (PTSD) that grew out of the war. These are interspersed with the main story, and I believe they can help one to view my experience a little better. I published several of the posts at my website, *Contoveros.WordPress.com.* ("Contoveros" was my father's name until someone at Ellis Island changed Pop's name to "Contos." Incidentally, Contoveros means "singer of truth" in Latin.)

So here is my story. It's meant for those among you that might gain some understanding of what war has done to someone who was drafted and led an infantry platoon in the war. I present it with the little wisdom and compassion my two messengers tried to instill into me and with my limited skills as a storyteller.

I am tired and sick of war. Its glory is all moonshine. It is only those who have neither fired a shot nor heard the shrieks and groans of the wounded who cry aloud for blood, more vengeance, and more desolation. Some of these young men think that war is all glory, but let me say…war is all hell.

—American Civil War General
William Tecumseh Sherman

PART I

RECALLING VIETNAM WAR DAYS AND NIGHTS

I had a premonition that something bad was going to happen on the morning that would become the worst day of my life.

It was hot. We had walked from a densely covered forest land until we came to the river and followed its banks to a secluded area with fewer trees but much larger bushes. I had ordered the platoon to set up a site to sleep nearby the night before. I would generally let the more experienced fellows—those from the Deep South and the West—suggest a spot to rest. They knew the way of the land back home, and in this place we called the "bush," the forests in which we spent fourteen days at a time patrolling and looking for any sight of the Viet Cong, if the farm and country boys felt it was a secure place to ward off an attack and remain out of the vision of the enemy, then it was good enough for me. As a city boy, the only outdoor encampments I ever set up were with the Boy Scouts of America, spent at overnight jamborees in Valley Forge National Historic Park, about twenty miles outside of my Philadelphia, Pennsylvania, home.

We settled in where one of the Southern boys suggested we stay. We had been shelled earlier that same day. We couldn't even fight back as the rounds of artillery exploded around us, forcing us to hit the ground looking for cover. There was no cover. There was no entrance to any cave, any type of crevice in the ground, or even any roadside culvert. We were in South Vietnam, some one hundred miles out of Saigon, embedded with the Twenty-Fifth Army Division.

Our own troops—artillery specialists with the US Army—had been shelling the area and missed their target, with rounds falling short and smashing into the earth where we had just walked during a routine mission. How do you fight such an attack? You cannot, and you quickly remember how you used to pray when you were a lot more connected to a Source above you, around you, and, most importantly, within you.

I felt helpless. As the first lieutenant, the one to whom I believed my troops looked for guidance and leadership, I could do nothing but cover my head with both hands and get into a near-fetal position, rolling myself into a ball to give the blast effect less of a target to damage.

I wanted a shovel so badly. I would have dug into the ground. I'd have dug into the earth beneath me with all the strength my impotent joints would have allowed me. Let me do something! Anything was better than just waiting for the next blast to hit closer. I realized then that the only digging device I had was shoved away in my backpack. It was a spoon, a spoon I prayed would enable me to dig and dig and dig. I'd dig so deep I'd create a foxhole and climb in for cover.

The bombing stopped after what seemed like one of the longest moments of my life. At times like these, I was certain the Angel of Death would march me out of the woods and into a different world. I wasn't ready for that. I don't know anyone who ever is, except for some saints or lamas I'd meet years later.

I thought I'd died for sure in that final moment, only to realize that I'd never left my body. My consciousness remained open and acutely aware of everything around me. My body grew still, as still as my breath, which seemed to finally return to normal. For a brief time, my heart and breathing had seemed to stop. It was scary, plain and simple.

Allow the president to invade a neighboring nation, whenever he shall deem it necessary to repel an invasion, and you allow him to do so whenever he may choose to say he deems it necessary for such a purpose, and you allow him to make war at [his] pleasure.

—Abraham Lincoln

NOTHING FRIENDLY
ABOUT FRIENDLY FIRE

We all lived through the friendly fire episode with nary a scratch to our physical bodies. Our psyches had been temporarily bombarded, and we might feel the residual effect of the blast's explosions decades later during times of stress. A few, like me, would relive that moment through what psychologists call a "flashback."

After the shelling, I forgot most of the promises I'd made to God if He'd only get me through this hell. I may have offered to become a Catholic holy man or at least one of those ushers who'd pass the collection basket around to help the poor in spirit who gathered in church when I was a kid. I'm surprised more guys didn't lose control of their bladders under such a strain. I remember, however, a young fellow from Louisiana who served as a radio operator. He peed himself during his first firefight. He wasn't too proud to mention it to his platoon leader, and I respected him for being honest about the fear we all felt during an attack.

⋏   ⋏   ⋏

On this day, which would become the worst one of my life, I had a different fear, a fear that the artillery shelling might not have succeeded the day before I took the platoon toward the nearby river. I wanted more rounds to blanket the spot just across the river where we were going to cross. I believed something or someone waited for us. I felt a trap had been laid and we were going to walk right into it.

I had been "in country" about four months and had fought in several fire-fights by this time. Adrenaline would rush through me, for example, as we'd move to secure a hole in the ground leading to a tunnel or to fall back from shots fired by a sniper we couldn't see who had gotten us in his sights. On at least one occasion, I had to prevent a soldier from desecrating the body of a dead Vietnamese killed by us. There was at least one man who wore in his "boonie hat" the bones from an ear he claimed was taken from one of the fallen Viet Cong. Not once did we come face to face with or engage in hand-to-hand combat with the enemy. There were no John Wayne–type skirmishes in the triple-canopy jungle we patrolled. We were lucky, and up until this day, no one in the platoon had been injured.

I felt calmer as we walked closer to the river. The calmness was almost palpable and eerie. I didn't like it. I wanted to shake this feeling I had and decided to call in mortar fire before crossing. How ironic that was! Mortar fire would lead to the worst day of my life, and before leaving Vietnam, it would figure highly in what I look back on as one of the best days of my life.

The men in my platoon called me "LT," short for "lieutenant," and I liked hearing them use the word. It showed a familiarity and camaraderie I wanted to share, even though officers were not supposed to fraternize with so-called enlisted men. Hell, weren't we all enlisted men to begin with? It wasn't as if I were going to have a beer with them or go out partying when the workday ended. I wanted them to know that I was just as much a "grunt" as they were and that I wouldn't ask them to do anything that I wouldn't do, which included walking point, which I did on several occasions. I even cut a path through over-grown jungle growth when there was no path and you needed a machete to clear your way through. It was nothing I would want to do on a daily basis.

War will exist until that distant day when the conscientious objector enjoys the same reputation and prestige that the warrior does today.

—John F. Kennedy

TRAINING FOR WAR EXHILARATING AT TIMES

Iknew next to nothing about war except for what I trained for in the United States. You had to learn to deal with pain while in Officer Candidate School (OCS) in Fort Benning, Georgia. You took punishment—which sadistic training officers called their form of training—without complaining. The six months I spent, through August 22, 1969, were the most rigorous of my life, which included "jump school," where I learned to "stand up, hook up, and shuffle to the door" while en route to exiting a C-140 airplane or a jet. You have to be a little bit crazy to want to go airborne. I wanted to toughen up myself in preparation for Vietnam, so I kissed my good sense goodbye as I leaped from a plane into the wild blue yonder.

Man was not meant to fly, but boy, could he float!

There is nothing quite like soaring through the air supported only by a parachute. It is exhilarating, and I felt I condensed a whole lifetime of living into those moments when I became one with the world, one with the universe while floating in the sky. It's an experience only those who ever jumped will ever know about. Some would even say it was better than sex on a Saigon Saturday night.

My parachute automatically opened as the hookup, some sort of a device, pulled whatever cord needed to eject the chute from my back. I had no time to think of the consequences of a mishap. Even if I got scared and wanted to back out while still onboard, there was an army instructor specifically trained to stand by the door and gently—or not so gently—shove you out.

▲   ▲   ▲

That first jump was a delicious taste of freedom from all, while it was also a uniting of all. I was free of all concerns and desires once I realized the chute had successfully opened, and I felt as if I were one with everything around me—the sky above, below, and all around. Everything was of me, and I was of everything!

The jump seemed to go on forever, and nothing mattered as the meaning of life appeared as close to me as the spare parachute on my chest. I knew somehow that I was connected with parts of the earth and the earth was connected with parts of me.

I began to steer my chute, pulling cords this way and that way, going left when I'd pull to the right and right while pulling left. I could also go forward and backward, depending on how I manipulated other cords. It made me feel like an eagle, in charge of my flight and my destiny while in the air, and I felt unique among all people to have been chosen to experience this thrill.

There was no discomfort or sense of feeling ill at ease. I felt mostly a sense of euphoric giddiness, particularly when the chute had opened to its full capacity with no lines cutting through the middle of chute, causing what airmen called a "Mae West." That would be a chute that appears like a gigantic bra, nicknamed for the 1930s glamour star. Such a twisting of lines could cause you to accelerate faster to the ground and possibly end up killing you.

Jumping had a spiritual component to it; at least I felt it did. It gave me a feeling of compassion for life below me. I was no different from anyone. We all were seeking happiness in one form or another, and I was just lucky enough to find that excitement and happiness could culminate by being in the air. I want to put quotes around the word "being" because you don't have any thoughts of the past or the future but live completely in the present when you're up there. Anyone could do this, could allow their hearts, minds, and spirits to take off and soar above the treetops while gliding thousands of feet above the earth's crust. There you might see how utterly insignificant we are, yet we are also so important you realize there must be a plan and a design that nature intends for us to uncover.

▲   ▲   ▲

I was supposed to have touched the ground lightly with the bottoms of my feet and then rolled onto my side, allowing my hips and legs to absorb some of the impact. Instead, I landed standing straight up! This was a no-no in military training. Too many inexperienced jumpers broke a leg by not rolling, and this was drilled into us during the three-week training session to become a parachutist.

I felt I had injured one of my legs. It was not a break or even a sprain but soreness from the jolt the leg took. I started to hobble while getting my chute together and retrieving it for the next packer, wincing as I put pressure on the leg. I limped but tried my best not to show it as I noticed an instructor approach and ask if everything was all right.

"Yes," I lied, not wanting to be barred from jumping again due to an injury. You needed a total of five jumps ("cherry jumps") in order to earn your wings. Wings are the medal awarded to jump-school graduates who become one of the elites of infantry servicepeople prepared to parachute into enemy territory should the need of the military require it. Hence, I jogged off the landing field, pain shooting up through my leg each time I made contact with the ground.

You run everywhere you go while in Airborne School. Many of the less physically able are weeded out during the course, as well as on the first day, which is what happened to me. I was a decent runner. Once I ran a mile in six minutes and eighteen seconds, just shy of the six-minute mark that would have given me a perfect record for the physical training course. Even with that record, I scored the highest in my platoon in OCS.

I had never run before being drafted. But I was in good physical shape despite smoking from the age of twelve. (I'd continue to smoke until April 9, 1996. That's when I got sick from what I can only believe was a mild stroke that went untreated.) From ages nineteen through twenty-two, I was able to withstand and endure pain. I could have put up with physical, mental, and emotional hits, having grown up Catholic and exposed to teachings that suffering was good for the soul and that the more you could bear with suffering in this world, the greater your reward would be in the next one.

So I ran through the discomfort and wheezing of the breath. If I had caved under the first painful irritation, I could have ended up like some of the overweight fellows on the sides of the road, the ones who were out of shape and looked down upon by the more athletically gifted.

I pushed through the pain and found a second wind. I discovered a higher level, allowing me to physically endure. I do it today while treadmilling and swimming. But it was different my very first day of jump school, and I dropped out of a three-mile run because I could not keep up the grueling pace. I had not gone that distance for more than a year when I was in my best physical shape while at OCS more than a year earlier, in 1969. Too many cigarettes, too much beer, and too many hours of sitting around took their toll on my twenty-one-year-old body, and I became "recycled." The army pushed my training back an additional three full weeks in order for me to get back in shape for the next Airborne School. I made the three-mile run, having been able to jog my way back to health during that period. The rest is history.

A   A   A

"Wait a minute! What about becoming an Army Ranger? You were accepted for Ranger School, weren't you?"

Yes, I was to start the school right after my Airborne training, but since I flunked out the first day of jump school and was recycled, I did not have enough time to become a ranger and still serve a full year in Vietnam. I got extra leave time, which enabled me to bring my girlfriend from Louisiana home to see me off. My mother suggested I marry this wonderful Cajun woman and, suffering from something called "war fever," we went before a justice of the peace and tied the knot. (Eight years later, following a subsequent divorce, I wondered if Ranger School would have been a better alternative, particularly since the marriage did not work out in the long run.)

I know not with what weapons World War III will be fought, but World War IV will be fought with sticks and stones.

—Albert Einstein (1879–1955), physicist and professor

A TASTE OF HEAVEN OFFERED HERE ON EARTH

https://contoveros.com/2010/09/25/a-taste-of-heaven-offered-here-on-earth/amp/

Pizza pie and a chocolate milkshake!

Each drew me like an oasis draws a man walking alone in a desert.

But it was no sandy desert I remember traversing. It was the triple-canopy jungle of Vietnam, where the hot, humid temperatures would compete with any Saharan sun blistering my throat, parched lips, and dry mouth. And I was not alone but leading a platoon out of the bush, where we survived another fourteen days and looked forward to three days of rest in a rear encampment.

To hell with Mom's apple pie and ice-cold lemonade. This city boy, raised in a melting pot called Philadelphia, wanted nothing less than ethnic foods made by ethnic hands.

Pizza with pepperoni! Hot with cheese that stuck to the slice as you tried to pull it apart, stretching the yellow substance as if it were taffy. Further and further in the air, the strip of cheese would get slimmer and slimmer until it snapped, and you made sure you got every little piece of it and didn't leave it in the tray for someone else to devour. You worked for that. You earned it. Remember how hot it was? It might have even burned your finger, manipulating it with your hand and not a fork or a spoon. Who ate pizza with utensils anyway? You fought for that slither. You suffered a pain, no matter how slight, to get that extra mix of mozzarella cheese.

And now you slowly place it into the mouth. Oh, that first bite! It was almost heavenlike. Hell. It was heaven, wasn't it? Particularly if you closed your eyes and let the taste mingle with your tongue, your teeth munching away, and your taste buds awakening to flavor of Italy…a touch of the old country, a hint of a big, loving, abundant Italian mama!

And then a delicious milkshake made the old-fashioned way, not some McDonald's rip-off. You needed the liquid mixture of milk, ice cream, and whatever other ingredient the Jewish deli served up. Or one made by a young pharmacist's assistant at a drug store with a soda fountain. Like Mrs. Kaplan, the spouse of the local pharmacist, who'd create such joy in the Brewerytown section of Philadelphia (Twenty-Eighth and Master Streets). There was nothing quite like the anticipation for that delicious drink. She'd use a long metal cup fashioned for a special heavyweight blender with three different speeds. No such thing as nonfat milk or nonfat ice cream when it came to a milkshake. Pour in a little chocolate syrup, and you slowly churn it all together at low speed. Next, hit a switch to get it moving quicker at medium, and then finally approach that high speed where the whirling sound assured you that you were about to be served a nectar a Greek god would offer a kiss from the love goddess Aphrodite to experience. (Or a kiss from the war god Ares, for you young ladies!)

It's what got me through the war. I mean that! Exposing myself and twenty-five other guys to firefights had nothing to do with halting the spread of Communism. Hell, I kinda liked the idea of a society where all were equal and shared our goods equally. (Polish sausage, German salami, Swiss cheese, Lebanon bologna, Italian sausage and salami, English muffins, Greek olives, Danish pastry, French fries, and Canada Dry ginger ale are just a few of the internationally named products I'd fight for.)

George Orwell's book *Animal Farm*, however, showed us some animals would become "more equal" than others. That was particularly true when spirituality was removed from a country, thus inhibiting the love and compassion people could have for all of humanity.

So I fought for pizza and milkshakes. Rather, the right to enjoy pizza and milkshakes despite outsiders' having no business being in places like Vietnam (Americans) and Afghanistan (Russians). Not unless you're seeking a trading partner to introduce a new food or drink. Can we all say Chinese egg rolls? Japanese sake?

▲   ▲   ▲

Musings like these got me through the long days and nights in Vietnam. Not all thoughts were of danger or what might be hidden around the next bush, tree, or path. I'd fantasize about the future and where my life might lead me a year, five years, or even ten or twenty from then! I never thought, however, that it would be forty years before I could safely return to my life in the jungle and recollect what I had tried for my entire adult life to suppress.

It's always much easier to look back on an event when it's over, no matter how difficult it really was the first time around. Just think about what I just said and try it out: take a major life event and think about it later, long after it happens. What the hell do we really know at age eighteen, twenty, or twenty-two? We're barely out from our parents' home and protection and seeing the world for the first time through tender eyes and tender hearts. What perspective could we possibly have? It is only when life hardens us a little that we can look at events fully and see them for what they really are.

Please join me in a brief look back on the Vietnam War before and after the worst day of my life tainted and colored my outlook toward good and bad, rich and poor, and saint and sinner.

I hate it when they say, "He gave his life for his country." Nobody gives their life for anything. We steal the lives of these kids. We take it away from them. They don't die for the honor and glory of their country. We kill them.

—Admiral Gene LaRocque

FAST FORWARD: QUESTIONS AND ANSWERS ON VIETNAM WAR

(The following questions were posed by Emily S., a sophomore at Creekview High School in Canton, Georgia, who was doing a project on the discrepancy between the treatment of Iraq and Vietnam veterans. During her research, she said she stumbled across a blog post I wrote about the Vietnam War while on a retreat at Omega Institute attending the Hidden Cost of War workshop. The blog post helped, she said, but she had more questions. The above interview was conducted by email on April 28, 2010. The following is the URL: https://contoveros. com/2010/04/29/answers-to-questions-about-vietnam-war/.

How did you feel when you realized you were drafted into the military?

I actually "pushed up" my draft after realizing I couldn't get out with a deferment due to a bad back. Had X-rays done but to no avail. I was just what Uncle Sam was looking for, a 1-A classification.

After notifying the draft board and getting a report date, I asked the board to delay my entry so that I could go in the draft two weeks later with one of my good friends from the neighborhood, someone I sang street corner harmony with in Philly. We ended up doing basic training together and met up more than a year and a half later in Fort Polk, Louisiana, him as a sergeant and me a lieutenant. He had just come back. I was about to go to Vietnam. *Did you support the war or were you against it?*

Did not care for war but did not protest it. I did join Vietnam Veterans Against the War in college after the war but took no active role. I just paid the membership fee to help end the war but took no part in marches, protests, and so on.

What did your friends and family say when you told them you had been drafted?

My oldest brother was a "lifer," one who made a career out of the military, so my family was used to having a soldier in their midst. It helped him, and I know being drafted and entering the army helped to straighten out a lot of issues I had at age nineteen.

Were they supportive?

My mother and father did not have much to say when I went in. My brother guided me toward OCS, the Officer Candidate School in Fort Benning, Georgia, after learning that I qualified. I guess someone saw some leadership qualities in me. I did say one of my heroes was Alexander the Great and that I believed that one person really could make a difference in life.

What was the general reaction you received from people once you returned?

I wanted to avoid people when returning home. Robert DeNiro captured my feelings in the movie *The Deer Hunter* when his character returned from Vietnam and stood in the hills of a working-class Pennsylvania town, looking down at the tavern where friends were planning his welcome home party and wanting no part of it. No one who has not been in the Vietnam War could ever understand that we did not want or believe we warranted any type of a hero's welcoming. At least, I did not think of myself as worthy. Don't know if it was due to the media, the general opposition to the war, or a sense of failure, having battled so many of my own demons while in Southeast Asia.

Were there any particular reactions that stood out to you? If so, what were they?

My second-oldest brother, John, picked me up at the Philadelphia airport just a few days out of Vietnam, and he drove the speed limit on the area highway. I wanted to shoot him but instead yelled and screamed, demanding that he slow down from the fifty-five miles per hour he was driving, not being used to such "reckless" speeds and having survived the previous year in Vietnam by being cautious.

I enrolled in a community college. I even attended a "sensitivity" session, or orientation session, at the school before classes began. Sat on a floor in a circle with guys with hair down to their shoulders and young girls who loved how the long-haired guys looked and spoke. Talk about cultural shock! Thank God for a vets club we founded on campus my first year back. It got me through it.

Do you think the government was supportive toward the Vietnam vets?

No. The military and the government did not understand the need for closure or debriefing. We needed time to adjust to a civilian world we had put behind us in order to survive the war. We lived primarily with "survivor skills" that no longer fit in. We still retained the fight-or-flight instinct and detested running away from something that scared us off. I "got myself up" to fight a lot. Still do. Only in the past several years have I learned to contemplate my next action when facing an anxious moment, but my first reaction has been to *act*, not to freeze with indecision or immobility.

Do you think that the general population was supportive toward the vets?

People in the general population either feared the Vietnam veteran or forgot him. They did not want to dwell on the Vietnam War, something which most deemed a failure. The biggest losers were us: the soldiers, marines, sailors, and airmen who put on the uniform only to face near ostracism on our return. Society refused to acknowledge the pain of losing—the colossal mistake our government made—and tried to deaden the pain we represented by intentionally pushing the veteran off its radar screen. The fear and wariness were fanned by the media. "Crazed Vietnam Veteran" was the headline inserted by newspaper copy editors when a reporter dug up a story about a vet committing a crime. Mostly, all vets were seen as killing machines (think Rambo), even though only a few served in combat.

It got to the point where veterans left their military service off their résumés. Keeping it there did more harm than good when trying to get a job.

Why do you think the Vietnam War was so unpopular?

There was an orchestrated effort by the most compassionate and highly intelligent segment of our society to end our nation's longest war. Done for the best intentions, it had disastrous results. The move to end the war was led by doctors, mental health experts, and liberal-thinking professionals who joined together to paint the war as different from any in the history of the United States. Before mental health agencies established PTSD and its predecessors "shell shock" and "battle fatigue," they came up with a separate and unique name for the rage, anger, and lack of impulse control Vietnam veterans faced upon their return: "post-Vietnam syndrome." They made this war out to be somehow different from all the other wars, as if there was something more horribly atrocious about this conflict than any other. "Baby killers!" spewed from the mouths of only a few but was heard by the ears of many, including those of us returning from war.

Lt. William Calley was convicted of doing no more than what a few of General Sherman's officers had condoned about one hundred years earlier. "War is hell" is what we learned about Sherman's March through Georgia and the ugly underbelly of war. "Hell is war" is the ugliness we had to learn from the army's cover-up of cold-blooded murder and the inability of a young officer to control his troops during a skirmish later called the My Lai Massacre. Lieutenant Calley was the only one convicted of war crimes out of all who fired weapons on the three hundred–some women and children plus a handful of elderly men in the small village area. The investigation showed many of the dead were sexually abused, beaten, and tortured, and some of the bodies were found mutilated. The worst offense imaginable helped to turn most Americans against the war, but some politicians wanted a "peace with honor" and delayed the inevitable for years.

Do you think that people during the 1960s had a realistic view of the war?

Americans knew only what our generals wanted them to know, and that came through the daily briefings in the safer rear areas where war correspondents were kept away from the real war events.

How did being in the war change your perceptions of it?

I never fought for God, Mom's apple pie, or anything patriotic. I only fought for my men, the guys beside me, in front of me, and behind me. I fought even harder and wanted revenge when a buddy got hurt. But I think I'd feel the same way if I were in a battle at home and not in a foreign land.

Did you participate in antiwar rallies once you returned? If so, did people ostracize you because you were a veteran?

Never took an active part against those still in the service. Joined and gave money for antiwar causes but took no active role.

Do you think people's views of Vietnam veterans have changed in the past forty years? How so?

People have forgiven themselves and their veterans for the mistakes our country made. I wish we could admit to mistakes we are still making in the wars we wage today.

Do you think that the Iraq veterans can relate to the Vietnam veterans? Why?

Yes. We share the same confusion one faces in war when one doesn't know who the enemy might be. Sometimes, unfortunately, it can be a villager standing in front of you or a youngster (you learn later) playing with a booby trap or drawing a soldier to a spot where an explosive device lies.

What words of advice would you give to Iraq veterans?

Keep the childlike innocence with you. The world ain't all bad. Someday you'll be able to enjoy the good in life and be free of nightmares—most of the time, that is. That won't come for a few years. Maybe. That's if you seek peace both within and outside of yourself.

(Let's stay current and focus on the treatment I sought as a combat veteran with what would be diagnosed as PTSD. The following is an article about acupuncture and how I was first exposed to it for free on one Veterans Day decades after fighting in war.)

Peace demands the most heroic labor and the most difficult sacrifice. It demands greater heroism than war. It demands greater fidelity to the truth and a much more perfect purity of conscience.

—Thomas Merton, Catholic mystic monk

ACUPUNCTURE CALMS
A VETERAN'S WOES

https://contoveros.com/2009/11/14/
acupuncture-calms-stress-a-veterans-woes/

Needles punctured my ears for the first time in my life as I sought help for my Vietnam War injuries nearly four decades after my army discharge.

Acupuncture was being offered for one free session to veterans on Veterans Day 2010, and I appeared at the Won Institute in Glenside, Pennsylvania, to take advantage of the procedure. The practitioner, Ed Cunningham, was kind, offering me some cheese and crackers as we made small talk and I got ready for the event.

I sat in a regular metal chair that may have had some padding. The room was in a building where students earn master's degrees in various forms of meditation as well as acupuncture. (Any veteran and/or veteran's family could attend by contacting Won Institute at acupuncture@woninstitute.edu.) I cleaned my ears with a small alcoholic rub that was provided. As he was standing behind me, I could not see Practitioner Cunningham hold the needles, but I felt the first pinprick on my left ear. I believe three more needles followed, each slightly higher on the ear than the previous one.

After completing the other ear, a procedure that took all of two minutes, a needle was stuck in the top of my head, where I was told the chi rested. I think the needle was used to help energy flow well.

I felt just the opposite take place!

I felt sedated. Almost numb.

Not so much with my body but with my anxieties. I had none, and I felt their loss with a happy, sweet sorrow. Sorrow? Hell, I experienced a wonderful feeling of freedom. Freedom from PTSD and all other agitators!

Sedated. He could have taken my tonsils out, and I would not have cared. I could feel no harm, and I was as peaceful as I have ever felt through meditation.

And I did not have to wait long to reach this state of awareness. It came within sixty seconds of the last needle. Instructed to close my eyes like in meditation, I relaxed with nary a thought for some twenty-five minutes. I did not experience the same lightness as in a meditation. The relaxation was more palpable—heavier, so to speak. I was free of all worries about the past and/or the future and completely immersed in the moment, being one with my breathing and the contact my body had: feet to the floor, arms on my lap, and buttocks on the chair. Like in meditation, I felt a oneness with the physical properties I touched. A oneness with the comfortable temperature inside the room and the slight taste of salsa my taste buds still noticed from the snack I had consumed minutes earlier.

Nothing this good could go on forever, and I slowly opened my eyes. The practitioner was seated on one of the chairs. He had moved around while my eyes were closed, but the sounds he made adjusting a table or dropping a package did not bother me or my relaxation. They were simply part of an environment that was engaged with me and engaged with my ease and comfort.

One of the doctors who had opened this clinic some six years earlier had come into the room. We had chatted before in the waiting room. He was a native of South Korea and served in the medical corps in his homeland. As a captain, he outranked me, and I saluted him, wishing him a pleasant Veterans Day before leaving.

The procedure invigorated and energized me, while at the same time, I felt calm and peaceful the rest of the afternoon and night. Even now, several days later, I still can remember the sense of wellness I felt come over me with acupuncture. I hope to return to the institute for a possible follow-up procedure. You see, I have this bad back, and if more needles could help me, I will gladly offer it up as a pincushion.

Someone has to die so that President Nixon won't be, and these are his words, "the first President to lose a war…"

—Senator John Kerry of Massachusetts

WHERE IS THE BOY I LEFT HOME FOR WAR?

https://contoveros.com/2012/05/10/
where-is-the-boy-i-left-at-home-for-war/

I knew a boy
Who went to war
And left his home
Behind him.
I knew him well,
That boy was me.
And now I cannot
Find him.

A Vietnam veteran's tweak of a World War II sailor's song. The above poem was framed and hung on a wall of the psychologist who helped me and other veterans deal with PTSD.

War is fear cloaked in courage.

—General William Westmoreland

NOW HEAR THIS!
NOW HEAR THIS!

I will share with you something I have revealed only to my therapist, one, in the hopes of getting it off my chest, and two, hoping others who might read this could open up and relate to how hate can destroy you if you let it fester.

That's what I did for so many years until finally realizing the only person my hate had been hurting was myself. Hate, like anger, is like a burning rock that I tended to pick up and carry with me, fanning the flames over and over every time I thought of the injustices done to me.

The only person my hate burned, however, turned out to be me. But it took years of counseling and meditation to understand this and to offer some compassion for those I believed had triggered my ugly emotion.

TRANSFORMING HATE COMPASSIONATELY

I hated two people in my life. Both were men in authority who demanded but never got my respect. Both were Italians who had controlled the path of my life's journey from young adulthood into my middle-aged years.

I loathed them as much as I believed they loathed me and wished me ill. It's difficult to forgive them but, looking back, I can feel some compassion for their actions and try to understand why God had placed them in my life.

The first was Lt. Col. Ralph Salucci, the battalion commander that ended up relieving me of my command not once but twice while I served as an infantry platoon leader in the Vietnam War. The second was Judge Angelo Guarino, who torpedoed nine of the ten jury trials I argued in a nine-week span; three of the juries were back-to-back-to-back.

RELIEVE MYSELF OF THE JUDGE'S IRE

At one time, I wanted nothing more in life than to stand in line and piss on Guarino's grave. I despised him for interfering with the jury process and tilting the playing field so far in favor of the prosecutor. He was evil incarnate, this judge in the Philadelphia Common Pleas court system. No defense lawyer trusted him to be fair. You could not try a case before him without a jury, knowing his predisposition to find everyone guilty of something no matter how flimsily the prosecutor presented his case.

(How did I end up being a lawyer and serving twenty years as a public defender in Philadelphia? Well, it was almost by default. You see, I studied journalism in college and worked as a newspaper reporter for a small newspaper in Pottstown, Pennsylvania. I was bypassed for promotion to copy editor and put my energies into the union at the paper. (I couldn't spell a lick, but I could have used the pay increase.) I became shop steward and then head of the paper's local and eventually took a leave of absence to serve as a union organizer for the Newspaper Guild of Philadelphia. We held one election, sponsored by the National Labor Relations, and lost. Still wanting to help my fellow journalists, I entered law school to become a labor lawyer. But I got a D-plus in a labor law class, and I decided to practice in a field where I got a sturdy C-plus average, criminal law. I once tried ten jury trials in the span of nine weeks. Some lawyers never try that many jury trials their entire lifetimes.)

Guarino had no "reasonable doubt." Reasonable doubt is the type of doubt that would make a reasonable person pause or hesitate before making a major decision in their life. Examples given by criminal defense attorneys included a doubt one might have on a dry, sunny day when visiting a house they wanted to buy and seeing water in the basement. Another example was whether a parent would let their school-age child get onto a bus that the parent saw swerve and nearly collide with another vehicle before being brought to an abrupt stop by a substitute driver who smelled a little of alcohol.

▲   ▲   ▲

Do you have a doubt? Do you refrain from taking action with something of importance in your life?

"Now, here is where reasonable doubt really kicks in" is what I'd tell the jury. "If you had no qualms, then you would find my client guilty. You have no doubt. But if you hesitated before making that decision, then you have a doubt, a reasonable doubt, and you are duty bound to the oath you took to find my client not guilty."

Only once was I able to get this closing argument across to jurors. That was in my very first trial in which the jury found my client not guilty. In all subsequent trials, Judge Guarino would either interrupt or sustain an objection during this speech, sometimes even when the prosecutor had not even raised an objection!

JUDGE FOULED UP IMPEACHMENT EFFORTS

Guarino would screw me during my impeachment setup and the eventual "gotcha" moment when I'd nail a prosecutor's witness, using their own words against them. There's nothing more dramatic in a jury than when you can lock in a witness to testimony they provided the prosecutor only minutes earlier with a statement they gave under oath in another court setting where they testified to the complete opposite of what they're now claiming was the truth.

"He's talking out both sides of his mouth," I'd argue to the jury when showing the disparity. "Was he telling the truth then but not now? How do we know if anything he says is the truth?"

I disliked calling anyone a liar. Instead, I gave them the benefit of the doubt, claiming they were confused or uncertain.

"But if they're confused or uncertain about one fact," I'd say, "how can you be sure they're not confused or uncertain about the other facts?"

▲   ▲   ▲

I won the first trial in which I impeached a police officer with his own testimony. My client, a young African American male, was facing a minimum of three years in prison for his first offense, and I believe his testimony, which came across credibly, helped to secure an acquittal with the impeachment of his one and only accuser, the cop. I believe justice was done.

That was the last time I was successful in impeaching a witness, however. Judge Guarino would once again interrupt my line of questioning and actually make faces to the jury as if he couldn't believe what was coming out of my mouth. I was too young and inexperienced to place his antics onto the record in most of the cases. Eventually I did, but unfortunately, what I put onto the record with much fear and trepidation had no effect in a subsequent appeal.

The appeal occurred a year later, after I had presented a defense witness to testify to an alibi for her son, who was the criminal defendant. "Alibi" is a word I never liked, and I tried not to use it. It is based on the Latin for "somewhere else," but I always viewed it with suspicion. Like many people, I believed that you didn't need a so-called alibi if you really hadn't done anything. An alibi was for those who needed one to prove something that may or may not have taken place.

"Stick to the facts!" Guarino shouted, cane upraised in his hand in the direction of the witness on the nearby witness stand. This was in full view of the jurors seated a few feet away.

The judge shocked me and the entire courtroom when he took over my redirect examination of the witness. Shouting at her, Guarino said, "Stick to the facts, madam."

That was bad enough, but he had also raised the cane he used to walk to and from court. He waved the cane in the witness's direction in what I could only view as a threatening manner. I objected on the record, speaking while still in shock, saying something to the effect of, "Objection. Argumentative."

I should have said, "The judge was badgering the witness with his cane," and gone into as much detail as I have in explaining this bizarre incident, which, needless to say, resulted in a guilty verdict.

⋏　⋏　⋏

Guarino was a defense attorney before becoming a judge. He knew the art of lawyering, particularly the science involved in jury trial work. A lawyer is not necessarily dealing with the absolute truth of the facts. The lawyer works with the appearance of those facts and knows how human nature will view them through certain lenses. A good defense lawyer can present the lenses for a juror to see the facts the way the defense lawyer sees them and then act accordingly with a more just verdict. Disrupting any one of several steps needed to create this jury perspective can be critical. Guarino knew this and would insert himself into the process, shattering any attempt for the defense lawyer to get their view of the facts across to the jury untainted and undisturbed.

I won three out of the nine cases I tried before Guarino. Of the six cases I lost, three were overturned in favor of my clients.

I left Guarino's courtroom in 1990. I had served as a Philadelphia public defender starting at the age of forty. Years later I heard that he had been removed from the bench for one of the nasty punishments he imposed on someone he thought was trying to dodge jury duty. Guarino would single out persons requesting jury exemptions due to hardships. If he believed the hardship was made up, he'd excuse them from being empaneled on the jury but issue a subpoena for them to appear in court as an audience member for the duration of the trial. Yes, they'd have to sit for days watching the jury trial rather than taking part in the process. Some trials would last a full week.

Guarino was warned not to do this by a higher court that some folks had complained to. He must have suffered a major disgrace when he was taken off the court bench in the middle of a jury trial where he had forced a doctor to return to his courtroom despite the physician's stated, on-the-record hardship. Guarino appealed the Pennsylvania Supreme Court ruling. I gave him only six months to live when his subsequent appeal was heard and denied by the Third Circuit Court of Appeals.

He died then, six months to the day. I had believed he had nothing to live for outside of his Philadelphia courtroom, and this proved it.

▲   ▲   ▲

I never made it to his grave site. From my perspective as a defense lawyer trying to get his client off from a crime he was accused of committing, I know what Guarino did was wrong. No, I was never that cynical. You see, I had believed and still believe that the role of the judge and the court is to provide justice. That means justice for both sides and not just the side you'd like to support and to see win.

Guarino was loved by prosecutors, police officers, and every person victimized in crimes committed against them. And while he tilted his court in favor of the Commonwealth—that is, the State of Pennsylvania—he tempered his final orders with sentences that were always fair. Guarino never imposed a maximum sentence in any of the cases I tried. Nor did he sentence anyone consecutively, that is, ordering someone to serve one five-year sentence after another five-year sentence.

I cannot forgive him, but now I can understand him a little and be a little more compassionate. And I stopped hating him within a few years of his death in 1994.

YOU NEVER FORGET YOUR FIRST HATRED

I have had more difficulty in offering compassion for the other bane of my existence, the battalion commander that caused decades of misery in my life. He must have had some redeeming features, but I never learned of them. I don't hate him anymore. That ended following years of counseling for anger management and PTSD.

The odd thing about Lt. Col. Ralph Salucci is that he was one of a half dozen or so battalion commanders I dealt with during my three-year stint in the army. I have blanked out the memory of all of them except for Salucci.

The first high-ranking officer I was assigned to serve under was a battalion commander. I was what the army called a "holdover" following basic training in Fort Bragg, North Carolina. My transfer or advancement to Advanced Individual Training was held up due to a delay in an investigation for my secret clearance. One could not be commissioned an officer without such a security check, and I learned after a year's delay that my father's past record or lack thereof may have caused red warning flags to be raised.

My father, Achilles Contoveros, left the tiny island of Nisyros when he was fifteen. (He could have been thirteen, depending on which Social Security card information you believe. He had two of them and two different dates of birth, but I'm not sure which, if any, is accurate.) He either "jumped ship" when his boat docked in the New York harbor or came through Ellis Island.

I never joined Ancestry.com and have had no access to the records nearly a hundred years old.

Nevertheless, young Achilles, who spoke no English and had never gotten beyond sixth grade, found work in the restaurant business, working his way up from waiter and short-order cook to full-fledged chef. In the early years, there was a story that he was ordered at knifepoint to leave New York City, where he worked in a speakeasy. Three thugs forced him into the back of a car and drove him to the outskirts of New York, where he was thrown out at the New Jersey border. It turned out the chorus girl he was dating was the girlfriend of one Lucky Luciano, who didn't take kindly to young Greek fellows—or any other kind of fellows—encroaching on his lifestyle or what he considered to be his property.

Achilles, who had the alias of "Charlie West," is alleged to have done some time in Sing Sing prison, also of the New York City area. I have never confirmed this, but it had become part of the family lore. I later learned that he was no stranger to the drug trade. A section of the speakeasy where he worked offered small rooms or dens where pipes filled with opium were offered to select clientele seeking more than the run-of-the-mill gin or whiskey.

He was from that part of the world that prevented him from being inducted into the military during both of America's major wars of the twentieth century. Nisyros, mentioned by Homer in the epic the *Iliad*, was governed by Turkey at the time of the First World War. The United States was not on the friendliest terms with that country and suspected anyone from its borders might not provide true allegiance to America.

During the outbreak of the next world war, Nisyros was controlled by Italy, which had taken sides with the Axis powers before Germany turned on that country. I have heard stories about how the Italians refused to kill the men in the villages like the Germans had done in nearby Crete. One of my aunts had married an Italian soldier, possibly an officer, and in retaliation for the soldier's lack of punishment of the Greeks, ordered their son into battle and was never heard of again. So when US government officials began looking into my father's past, they apparently needed more time to find out he truly was an American who supported the American way of life.

I served the battalion commander for some two months, getting him coffee, accepting and passing on telephone messages, and every now and then raising and lowering the headquarters' flag. Don't ask me what he looked like or even his name. I couldn't remember if you paid me. I was then assigned top Advanced Individual Training at Fort Dix, New Jersey, where I was held over again because of the lack of a clearance. I met no battalion commanders there, and the next one I'd come into contact with was after I had finished Officer Candidate School and had completed a tour of duty as a training officer at a basic training unit in Fort Polk, Louisiana.

NOTHING IN COMMON WITH HIGHER-UPS

Again, I remember nothing except getting dressed in my army dress blues for some officers' event where I met and shook hands with the battalion commander and his wife, who stood in line with other higher-ups while all of us junior officers, friends, and loved ones paid our respects while bowing to 'em. Each and every one was a white male, I seem to recall. I had nothing in common with any of them.

Upon leaving Fort Polk, however, the battalion commander had gifted me with a letter opener in the shape of a bayonet and a metal mug with the name of the battalion and division engraved prominently on them. I learned later that he had offered these keepsakes to all junior officers. I still have them but have forbidden anyone to use them because I'm afraid they'd get lost with any daily contact.

I placed the bayonet on display beneath a set of medals I received from my tour of duty. Included in the display is a metal fork with an engraving on the back that shows how our country has dealt with our sworn enemy of yesteryear. The engraving says it was made in Vietnam, one of the newest trade partners with America.

I do remember a lieutenant colonel who wanted to see what life was like in the bush. The bush is the term we grunts used to designate our venture into the jungle lands and environs of South Vietnam. We'd "hump" the boonies—that is, engage in reconnaissance missions for two-week intervals. The boonies is another word for what we called the bush.

A newly appointed battalion commander wanted to see what spending a night on the jungle mission was like, and my company commander suggested the senior officer accompany my platoon on one of our missions. The senior officer was gray-haired and old. He reminded me of Kenneth Wright, my second wife's father, who taught music as a professor at the University of Kentucky while playing the violin in several orchestras.

No Stereotypical Warriors in 'Nam

In other words, the man looked kind and compassionate as opposed to fierce and warriorlike. Come to think of it, I don't know of too many of us grunts that looked like the stereotypical warrior. Most were civilians who had been drafted into the army and fought the hardest when attacked and pissed off by enemy fire.

Well, we saw no enemy fire during the two or three days that the head honcho spent with the platoon. I treated him with due respect but advised him to set up in the perimeter like any other trooper when camping at night. He never walked point and simply tasted the life of a typical foot soldier, a life that was pretty boring and mundane except for those days when combat interrupted your jaunt through the jungle.

That battalion commander had nothing but good things to say about the First Platoon in Charlie Company, my platoon. I don't know what happened to him, but the next commander that got assigned to us was the direct opposite. Ruthless and demeaning, Lieutenant Colonel Salucci would become the one and only officer I knew whose own men would try to kill him.

▲　▲　▲

The Other Man I Hated

Why did I choose to speak about the judge before addressing the colonel? I believe the one toughened me up for the other. Nothing that Judge Guarino could ever do or say could ever come close to the humiliation and shame Salucci caused me to feel. Who cared what names the judge called me? "Liar" was one of them, but in a more gentrified way, Guarino called me a "dissembler." At first I took some offense. I had no idea what it actually meant, but I knew it was not meant as a compliment.

A dissembler is a fake, a person who falsifies who he really is and purports to be someone else. Well, yes, I guess I was. I smiled at you, judge, but I didn't want to. I wanted to curse you. I showed you respect, not for your person but for your position as a judge. You see, I had contempt for you from the moment I tried my second case in front of you and you took sides with the prosecutor in a blatant attempt to ensure the defendant was seen in the light most unfavorable to his cause.

MY MEN UNDER ATTACK AGAIN

I saw the defendant as one of the many men I led in combat. I saw the people I deemed under attack by a system that pretended to offer a presumption of innocence but relied on the direct opposite: if you've been arrested, you must have done something. That's what most people I met believed, and without a lawyer standing up and shouting the correct view one should take, I feared the Guarinos of the world would always obtain dishonest convictions.

Yes, I'd fight like I was back in Vietnam, using my wit and limited resources to come up with defenses whenever the prosecutor would strike my guy with one piece of evidence or another. Somehow I'd minimize the evidence by cross-examining a witness with facts the assistant district intentionally left out. Many jurors picked up on this lack of candor, and little by little, I was able to get them to see the defendant not as someone totally foreign to them but someone like their brother, father, son, or in the case of women jurors, romantic partner.

RAISE REASONABLE DOUBT ALWAYS

In other words, they'd see them as humans (misunderstood soldiers), not someone one should rubber-stamp as guilty no matter what reasonable doubt might exist.

I'd fight, yell, scream, and beg if I thought it would help. I attacked one cop so severely, slamming my hand onto the jury box, that one judge banned me from trying jury trials in her courtroom ever again. Two judges kicked me out of their courtrooms, holding me in contempt until hearing from my supervisor about my conduct.

I didn't care. I wasn't going to let any one of my men get hurt or left behind if I could do something about it. No one was killed in the platoons that I commanded in Vietnam. No one was left behind. I looked out for the welfare of my men, and to hell with any authority figure who took umbrage with the way I achieved my set goals.

⟁ ⟁ ⟁

The first thing I noticed about the new battalion commander, Lieutenant Colonel Salucci, was how much he looked like a Roman emperor. There he was—a grossly overweight, dark-skinned Italian officer sitting on a cushioned chair in a makeshift war room with a full-scale, light-up map of the zone of operation behind him.

He reminded me of Nero, the emperor who was supposed to have fiddled while Rome burned during some period of history. And while such a burning is much worse than anything that happened during my time in Vietnam, Salucci seemed as standoffish and full of self-importance as any person I'd ever had contact with.

He spoke slowly, as if his every word carried immense meaning. Whenever he looked at anyone, he'd look down. He looked down on me. At least I felt he was always looking down at me and the other junior officers who gathered before him for our introduction to and indoctrination in the Salucci way of soldiering.

⟁ ⟁ ⟁

Salucci worked his way up through the ranks. He had fought in World War I and, unfortunately, saw many battles from the perspective of what we called "trench warfare." At many times he would tell us to dig in when setting up an encampment, forgetting that the army had not issued shovels to soldiers since World War II. He still thought in terms of the old ways, the ways that had kept him alive, and he was hoping for advancement from what we called a "light" colonel to a "full bird" colonel. The term "light" referred to the designation of a lieutenant colonel who was one pay grade below a full colonel and one pay grade above a major. Basically, he was like an assistant colonel.

But Salucci was looking at what could be his last hurrah. You see, he had been passed over twice for promotion. The higher command had refused to make him a full colonel, and if he was not chosen the next time his number was called, Salucci knew he'd be asked to retire.

In the Vietnam War, the most secure way for an officer to get promoted was through what was called the body count: the higher the number of people your men killed, the more favorably you'd be viewed by command central. That was particularly true with Salucci, who wanted more and more killings to survive in the only life he ever knew. If he was bypassed one more time and not promoted from lieutenant colonel to full colonel, then he would have to leave the army after having served as a private in World War I.

My goal in combat was not to kill but to simply get through each day of war without getting killed and to prevent all of my men from getting killed. In other words, I had a drafted man's mentality: get me through this one tour of duty, and I'd be done with war forever.

I became the least favorable junior officer Salucci commanded. I concurred with almost nothing he wanted from his men. Yet I suffered emotionally and mentally when I couldn't provide it, and he eventually relieved me of my command and fired me.

✝ ✝ ✝

I was in awe of Salucci from the very first time I saw him seated in the chair. I was sitting in a fold-up wooden one in the audience on the dirt floor. Salucci's chair rested on a platform some six to eight inches above the ground. You had to look up to him whether you wanted or not.

He reminded me of a slick and oily Sebastian Cabot, the English actor. Now, place a robe across his chest and pretend that you've been transported back to the Roman Senate, where a "back-bencher" senator would speak only to criticize and to cause disruption and disharmony, and you'd get a better idea of who Salucci resembled from my perspective.

"Out of Uniform" Due to Swollen Feet

He growled at me on seeing me. I later learned he had chastised my company commander for my unprofessional bearing. He claimed that I was "out of uniform" when meeting him and that I was lucky I didn't get a public admonishment.

I wore sandals to the meeting. Everyone else wore boots, the type of cloth boots that helped your feet to "breathe" in the hot and humid jungle. They dried quickly and helped soldiers prevent jungle rot to the feet.

Well, my feet swelled so much that I couldn't fit them in my boots after taking my boots off when entering the base camp from humping in the boonies. I had slept in a rice paddy, a pond on grass used to grow a rice crop, the night before, exposing my left arm to an all-night water submersion that would eventually cause me pain for the rest of my life whenever it would rain.

Water surrounded my feet too. Each foot was soaked throughout the night, so by the time I awoke, I could hardly walk without pain. I had spoken to a medic on my return to the camp in the rear, and rather than go on "sick call," I decided to tough it out by simply letting my feet dry out. Hence, I wore sandals to the meeting rather than boots.

But Salucci would not have cared. It's the appearance of officer propriety that counts, not the actual merit. Appearances, according to Salucci, meant more than substance.

I remember three separate incidents where Salucci left permanent scars on my psyche. The first was when as leader of the First Platoon, I had gotten word that the Third Platoon leader, Victor Lee Ellinger, had been shot. I saw Vic as a brother. He was one of only three junior officers in our company, and we carried the same worries and concerns for our mission and the welfare of our men. I looked up to him. He was southern-born and a natural leader. If you wanted to make a movie with a war hero in mind, you could not go wrong with choosing the blond-haired, blond-mustached Vic, whose charismatic bearing caused one and all to want to follow him and fight to the death for whatever cause he suggested was worthwhile.

FORCED MARCH THROUGH THE JUNGLE

When I heard he was shot, I went a little crazy. "Berserk" might be one way of describing my behavior. I ordered all my men to begin marching. We were more than a klick (a kilometer) away from where the Third Platoon had met enemy fire. I ordered my men to "quick step," or march quicker than the regular pace. I didn't know it at the time, but I soon took over as point man, the one to walk first. I was in such a hurry, I didn't want to have someone else lead the pace. I led the platoon through the jungle, forcing my way over bushes and around trees to get to a clearing, where I picked up the pace even more and began to move even more quickly at what we call "double time."

The only thing going through my mind was Vic. "I gotta get to Vic. I gotta help him. My men will rescue him. We'll save him. My God, don't let anything more happen to Vic. Help us to help him."

By the time we got to his location, Vic had died. I never saw him; I was too busy getting my men set up to defend the Third Platoon from any possible additional attacks. Vic's remains had been medevaced out by the time I thought to see his body.

He was not the only casualty that day. I caused two of my own men to suffer severe heat exhaustion during the forced march. They were also medevaced out for treatment. And I never got over the feeling of guilt that the sniper who killed Vic should have gotten me. I think they call it survivor guilt.

What did Salucci have to say about this? He criticized me for the formation my men marched while trying to come to Vic's aid. He had flown over the area in a Huey helicopter and saw my failed attempt at a rescue. He told me I should have ensured each man walked further apart from each other and that they were easier to pick off by the enemy while marching close to each other.

He was right, but in this context, he was also so wrong.

DECADENT LIEUTENANT COLONEL SALUCCI

When I think of the word "decadence," a vision of Lieutenant Colonel Salucci automatically comes to my mind. I'm not talking about decadence as in Marie Antoinette and the French King Louis XVI but an evil, slimy, living-off-the-labor-of-other-people type of decadence.

I don't know why, but I had been ordered to report to Salucci's bunker one night when my platoon had been resting in base camp. I made sure I was in full uniform, meaning headgear and footwear. I remember walking to the bunker. It was fully protected by what looked like hundreds of sandbags to protect it from a direct hit by enemy fire. It would be in this bunker that some soldier in one of our companies—one of Salucci's own men——would try to kill him by tossing a hand grenade at the bunker while he lay sleeping inside. The assassination attempt, or attempt at a coup d'état, ended harmlessly when the explosion failed to penetrate the bags and did no damage whatsoever to the metal culvert topping that encased his bunker.

I knocked on the door of the bunker and entered when a voice told me to come in. Inside were bright electrical lights, not lanterns, and a picnic-size table where Salucci and a major had been seated. I smiled, pretending that I was so pleased to be in their company, and took care of whatever business I had as soon as possible. It was just before I was leaving that the significance of what I was witnessing finally sunk in.

They were drinking champagne. I saw them toast with specially designed glasses after the major poured the sparkling liquid from what I took to be a champagne bottle. But that wasn't all. Salucci had actually told me that they were also eating caviar, as if he wanted me to know that he was a member of a higher class, a class which few foot soldiers could ever hope to gain promotion to.

He looked greasy and smarmy. I detested him right then and there. If he had touched me or come into physical contact with me, I don't think I'd ever be able to wash off the…I don't know, I guess you would call it the stench of his essence.

Here we were, hundreds of grunts in the companies he commanded in the Twelfth Infantry Battalion who ate mostly out of cans provided in C rations, and our leader was dining from caviar cans and champagne bottles. We were getting shot at and dying in the jungle while he was safe and secure in the rear area as a Rear Echelon Motherfucker (REMF). Oh, how I despised him.

Worst Christmas Day of My Life

Of course, Salucci figured prominently in the worst day of my life, which is part of what this manuscript is about. How many of us can pick out a moment in time when we can look back and say, "That's it; that's the worst and most dreadful thing I have ever seen, heard, or experienced in my life"?

Many, I bet, would point to a death of a family member or loving friend. It's the sudden loss of someone that can hurt. Loss can also be felt in a life situation, such as losing your job or losing the ability to live a life of your choosing. You get fired because you turned fifty-five, and no one will hire someone your age. You played the piano all of your life but can no longer suffer the pain in your hands, which arthritis has stiffened and mauled. Or you lose your sight as a traffic controller; you lose your hearing as a music critic; you lose your taste buds as a wine connoisseur.

The worst day of my life is recorded elsewhere in this book. It occurred in December 1970, about a month after Lt. Victor Lee Ellinger was shot and killed by a sniper. I was leading one of two of the squads I commanded as leader of the First Platoon. Five men got struck by mortar fire due to what Salucci deemed my negligence.

DRIED UP AND FINISHED AT AGE TWENTY-TWO

Salucci relieved me of my leadership role, and I lived in no-man's-land over a stretch of time that included December 25, the birthday of Jesus. I remember lying on a cot alone in some rear echelon environment. I had no feeling, no emotion, and I felt flat and used up. There I was: twenty-two years old, dried up and finished with life, wanting nothing more than to find a hole, crawl into it, and die.

I had failed. I had screwed up, and others paid the price for what I did or failed to realize would happen with my decision to call in the mortar fire.

I'll never forget how I felt lower than dirt, if that's possible. Nothing could improve my life, improve my situation. I'd survive and live despite this, but I would never forget that Christmas Day, one of the lowest points of my life. It haunted me and tainted the Christmas holidays forever after; something inside of me would prevent me from fully enjoying Christmas in the years that would come. No one I knew understood this unless they had had a similar Christmas past. Only the veterans who fought in combat on the Lord's birthday knew what had troubled me year after year. Many have told me of their own experiences about the holidays.

Salucci's firing caused me to feel like a failure in everything I would attempt for the rest of my life. I didn't know this was the case, but I would use this sense of failure to push me to extreme limits later. I had to be better to compensate for how little self-worth I had. I'd go to school and get a bachelor's degree in three years rather than the normal four years. I then got a master's degree in one year instead of the two-year program that most graduate schools required of their students. I had to excel, I felt, to make up for what I didn't do or didn't do right when I had the chance.

NO QUITTING WHERE SALUCCI IS CONCERNED

Salucci's face would come to my mind whenever I thought about quitting or giving in to fear, anxiety, or plain old tiredness in any scholastic endeavors. I pushed to get a job as a newspaper reporter, first with the college newspaper and then with a weekly newspaper. From there, I wrote my way onto one of the most respected small-town newspapers in America, the *Pottstown Mercury*, which is also the smallest paper in the country with more than one Pulitzer Prize in journalism to its credit.

I fought hard as a union contract negotiator at the newspaper and then as a union organizer for the Newspaper Guild, going off to law school to once again look out for the welfare of my men as a labor lawyer, only to change my life's career choice after getting a D in Labor Law. I found my true calling while overcoming that failure by becoming a public defender in Philadelphia.

I met each failure with a gritty determination to not give in to what I felt on that lowly cot back in Vietnam. Nothing that life threw at me in my later years would ever be as shameful and life draining as what I felt then.

Should I give thanks to Salucci today? Should I treasure him as a gem that has taught me to grow and seek a higher wisdom in life's experiences?

I don't want to forgive you, colonel. But maybe I can understand you a little better and thank God for the strength that He gave me to raise myself from that low point to a higher one. I now can feel blessed to have lived through the war and to have kept all of my men alive despite the unsuspecting and unforeseen casualties of all wars.

⋏　⋏　⋏

(The next story I wrote for my blog at Contoveros.WordPress.com concerns a mutiny that I had helped to "put down" after Salucci fired me a second time. I could have sat on my hands and done nothing to spite him and his chances for promotion, but I focused on my men and the harm they'd face if they continued with their disobedience of a direct order in a time of war, even if their actions were in direct support of me, their platoon leader.

I believed I did the right thing then, and looking back as I did in the article, which is another post for a blog, I believe it more so today.)

As far as I am concerned, war itself is immoral.

—US World War II general Omar Bradley

LIGHT SHINES ON MY MUTINY QUASH

https://contoveros.com/2009/11/18/finally-light-shines-on-my-mutiny-quash/

I lied to my platoon to prevent a mutiny while at war in Vietnam.

Some forty years later, I granted myself forgiveness. I cleansed a wound that had never seemed to heal until now.

I served as a first lieutenant in Vietnam and was relieved of my command of an infantry platoon just two hours before getting orders to appear at a helicopter base port. Taken by surprise, I met the battalion commander, Lt. Col. Ralph Salucci, who asked me to help avoid a military disaster from developing any further. My platoon of some twenty-five soldiers—grunts, as we liked being called—had refused to board the ships that would fly them into the field to patrol and engage the enemy. Most of the men sat on the heliport, reclining on their backpacks, disobeying all orders to climb aboard.

A day earlier several members of the second squad were medevaced to a hospital after being ambushed by the Viet Cong. I had assigned a sergeant with some ten years' experience to lead the squad. Unfortunately, he was "new in country" and may not have had time to become acclimatized to the situation. In other words, he didn't know what he was supposed to do in a war zone yet. He should have marched the men further away from the drop zone, where the Viet Cong had seen the helicopter's flight pattern.

Our superior officer blamed me, the man in charge, and for the second time in my young military career, I found myself removed of my command.

For some reason I was put in command of another platoon in the battalion. I guess the commander needed someone to fill in when the other lieutenant had left country. I was devastated the first time and view that period as the lowest moment of my life. I felt lower than dirt and less useful than the ground below. At least dirt could be used to grow things and offer a structure to build on, I believed then.

This time, however, my being sacked hurt far less. I knew I had done everything to ensure the well-being of my platoon and instill in each member an esprit de corps that carried over into their individual lives. They learned to live for each other, to work as a unit, and to place the needs of the platoon over their own.

It came as no shock when I heard they refused to go to the field! It was a mutiny, pure and simple. They protested what they believed was an outrageous act committed against them: the removal of their leader, 1st Lt. Michael J. Contos, yours truly.

There never was a good war or a bad peace.

—Ben Franklin, US founding father
and a Philadelphia printer

MY MUTINY QUASH CAUSES PRIDE AND SADNESS

https://contoveros.com/2009/11/18/my-mutiny-quash/

I had never felt so proud of anything—ever—as I was of their unselfish act of rebellion. For two hours they put themselves on the line. No, they didn't expose themselves to a firefight. (That would come later.) But they were willing to face military sanctions—Article 15s and possibly a court-martial—for someone they believed truly looked out for their welfare.

I ended up betraying their trust. I tried to convince them to end their holdout, to give up a fight they could not win. I could not agree with their arguments without showing a contempt and total disrespect for a superior officer, the battalion commander, who would be passed over and not promoted because of a low body count. He ended up relieving two out of the three young lieutenants in my company. The Viet Cong had shot and killed the third remaining junior officer.

I lied to this one young man I had cross-trained as a medic and a rifleman. He would fill in should we be unable to get to the regular medic who was assigned to the other squad. I remember speaking to him as if it were yesterday. He was from Brooklyn, New York. He reminded me of myself:

a lot of spunk for a small guy, along with a bit of a mouth and very little respect for authority.

"Tell me it isn't so," he said, that I wasn't let go and would continue to be their LT.

LOSING INNOCENCE AND INTEGRITY

Looking him in the eye, I told him what was needed to convince the others to get on the choppers and fly out of base camp. I said that I would accompany them. It was a lie. I lost a bit of innocence that day. I lost some integrity, a small part of my soul.

That has haunted me ever since...well, until tonight, when I meditated with a group and we focused on healing past moments in our lives. By using this technique, I was able, for the first time, to view this incident not with the eyes of a twenty-one-year-old, inexperienced young man but with the eyes of the "Higher Self." I knew what I did was right. As a matter of fact, I now know that I had the law to back me up, criminal law, which I have learned from twenty years of practice.

You see, the common law, now codified into state statutes as well as in military practice, allows for a defense when a person commits one criminal act to prevent a far more serious act from occurring. For example, you break into a house to rescue someone from a fire. If you had not committed a burglary, the one in the house might have died.

Had I not taken the action I did, my men would have faced punishment under military law and the possibility of dishonorable discharges. I can now say I would have done the same thing had I to do it all over again. Back then, however, I could not see that through the pain I felt. Nor did I have the wisdom to know the difference between one single principle and how an act of love, compassion, and understanding could provide for the good of the many.

(I like to think that a soldier's frame of mind is not created when entering boot camp or even when placed in harm's way in a combat zone. It starts early, perhaps as young as four or five, when a young person is faced with challenges and they choose to respond to those tests a certain way. Many of those tests can be character building, and it with this thought that I offer the next series of posts on name-calling.)

---

ded missiles and misguided men.

—Martin Luther King Jr.

NAME-CALLING GETS YOU KICKED IN THE END

https://contoveros.com/2010/01/28/
name-calling-can-get-you-kicked-in-the-end/

Patty DeMarco made me cry. He called me names and wouldn't stop as I tried to walk away, following me down the one-way street in North Philadelphia where we lived. On and on he went, badmouthing me, until he saw my brother, who helped me into his little red wagon and pulled it home, me sobbing all the while behind. I was four years old.

"Refugee" was one of the names Patty called me. "Deportee" was another. I didn't know what either meant, but he aimed the words at me and my family. I knew inside they were unkind words. They meant to hurt someone, to make fun of them, and to belittle them because they spoke a different language than you.

The potential bully-in-training then called me the worst name that a kid could call another in the aftermath of World War II: he called me a DP.

▲　▲　▲

The term "DP" is a legal one used internationally for a class of people displaced from their homelands by war or some tragic act of God. It was an abbreviation for "displaced person" that was used widely during the Second

World War to describe the refugee outflows from Eastern Europe. It was used to specifically refer to one removed from his or her native country as a refugee, a prisoner, or a slave laborer.

Most of the victims of the war, the political refugees and the "DPs" of the immediate post–World War II period, were Ukrainians, Poles, other Slavs, and Estonians who refused to return to Soviet-dominated Eastern Europe.

"DP" became the derogatory term nativists in the United States used against nearly everyone with foreign accents.

⋏　⋏　⋏

My father spoke with an accent. He was fifteen when he came from Greece, the eldest of nine boys and girls, while making his way in America during the roaring twenties. He came from a small fishing village on the island of Nisyros, a volcanic landmass split into four tiny villages.

Patty made fun of the way he talked. Patty also poked fun at the woman across the street that spoke with a German accent. He always said it in a way to make people feel bad. I felt bad for them as well as myself.

As I grew older, I heard other remarks, and while none made me cry, they hurt the same way. "Spic" and "greaseball" were among the hateful words I got called. And then there was the variation of the N-word, as in "n—— lover," used against me, and the full, ugly word against my friends who happened to be black.

Kids did not come up with those words by themselves. They heard them from their parents. The words got used at the dinner table by mostly poor white men who were just passing on the bigotry from their fathers and their grandfathers.

And it wasn't just the men. I dated a girl who let her bias show. We had argued and broke up. She called me a spic. I thought you had to be Spanish or of a Hispanic background before someone could call you that. This Irish girl knew next to nothing about the world but had learned enough from some source to call someone that name, whether it fit or not.

Some called me a "little Jew bastard." They had gotten my height down pat but my heritage and birth status completely wrong. But it didn't seem to matter—name-calling fed the fear and ugliness inside of them. It gave fuel to their little minds and their petty need to feel superior by putting down someone different from themselves.

▲   ▲   ▲

Calling a kid names could cause a lasting scar that kid may have to deal with later in life. It's either that or you learned how to toughen up, as I did, and let the wisecracks, the slurs, and the hate-filled and ignorant remarks simply glide over you.

I remember my teenage years and the names aimed at me by people I didn't know or hardly knew. On occasion I'd hear somebody call me queer. I'm not homosexual, "not that there's anything wrong with that," to quote the old *Seinfeld* bit. But I never shied away from such "feminine" activities as dancing and singing, getting "dressed up" for a party, and speaking in complete sentences and not the monosyllables used by a lot of so-called tough guys on the block of North Philadelphia where I grew up.

Later still, I got hit with such labels as "racist" and then "sexist." Neither fit, but I never stayed around those persons long enough to prove them wrong. They did not know me, and I was maturing enough to know my bending over backward to show them the opposite would be a waste of time. Theirs and mine.

▲   ▲   ▲

When it comes to name-calling, I'm not talking ancient history here. I remember returning from a trip to Greece in late 2008 and hearing a comment from a fellow Vietnam veteran twice my size about my countrymen. We were riding in an elevator full of veterans, and this Patty DeMarco type—a bully—asked me if I enjoyed myself with all the "Greek men" in Athens. It was a slur about Greeks and the acceptance of homosexuality from Ancient Greece.

"Yeah," I said as loud as I could. "Including your mama!"

It got a big laugh all around—except from the homophobic name-caller, who turned red in his lily-white face. He was the same one who said his parish priest had to "clean out" the Catholic Church recreational hall when a group of Muslims was permitted to hold a meeting there.

The guy's old, age-wise as well as culturally. He's got white hair, and we all know that he lives alone with his PTSD. Few of us veterans have had much, if anything at all, to do with him. I learned that he is also estranged from his own family, particularly a daughter about whom he had often moaned to us because she refused to have contact with him and she keeps the grandchildren separated from him.

When will he ever learn that you just can't elevate yourself? That you can't improve your lot by trying to tear down another because of their religion, their politics, or their way of life?

▲   ▲   ▲

The next time Patty DeMarco tried to call me a bad name, I kicked his ass from one end of Brewerytown to the other. Hit him as hard as I could, shouting, "Get up, shrimp boats!" as he fell to the pavement, cowering next to the marble steps leading to one of the row homes on our block. He held both arms over his face as snot poured out and onto his clothes. Now it was his turn to bawl.

The only name he called then was for his "mama."

It felt good, but I would not recommend it for an adult who picked up PTSD during a lifetime of stress and strain. They could end up in jail, while the name-caller could find themselves calling the city morgue their new home.

▲   ▲   ▲

I now know that no insult should ever be given in retaliation for some other insult; there should be no eye for an eye, no evil for another evil. We should try our best to understand that a person's hurtful remarks stem from ignorance. Not the book-learning or scholastic type of ignorance; it stems from their never being told or taught about something we more fortunate ones have been exposed to.

We, too, could find ourselves living in ignorance of something and would need the compassionate understanding of a kind and loving person who might one day (very gently and very skillfully) point out the error of our ways.

▲   ▲   ▲

"Sticks and stones may break your bones, but names will never hurt you" is how the saying goes. They may not hurt, but I don't think you ever forget them either. If you're lucky and have toughened yourself at a young age, you use them to either build character or learn how to forgive from a distance for harms done you a long time ago.

Neither shall they learn war anymore.

—Jewish and Christian Bibles. Isaiah 2:4; Micah 4:3

"LEST WE FORGET" NAMES CALLED SOLDIERS

https://contoveros.com/2010/01/29/
les-we-forget-names-called-our-soldiers/

N o one's ever called me "baby killer."
I never was spit on upon returning home to the United States following a year at war in Vietnam.

And while friends and coworkers I met through the years may have thought it, none have said to my face they believed I was one of those "crazed Vietnam veterans."

I'm grateful for never having to experience this in my life, particularly after wondering the other day about all the names people have called me while growing up. I forgot about my military life, the years I spent first as an enlisted man and then as a "ninety-day wonder" lieutenant in the army. I am now one of the veterans with time on their hands to reflect and ponder life, the good and the not so good.

I believe the term "baby killer" surfaced after Lt. William Calley, an officer serving in my old army division—the Twenty-Third Division, also known as the "Americal"—had led a platoon that decimated Vietnamese families in the village of My Lai. As a lieutenant, he was in charge of men who lost their humanity and killed indiscriminately, taking the lives of some three hundred people, mostly women and children as well as elderly men, with little or no proof they had anything to do with the killings of GIs days earlier or the possible aiding and abetting of the Viet Cong. It's true, some of the twenty-five men under Calley's command did kill babies. None was ever convicted of any crimes, save the young officer who ended his silence sometime in 2010 and offered his remorse for the actions of his platoon.

All servicemen seemed to have gotten painted with that broad brush by the media and America's collective consciousness shortly after the publicity of My Lai and its cover-up. No one pointed out what General Sherman had said a hundred years earlier, that "war is hell." I might add that war is hell for all persons: not only for those killed on both sides of the battlefield but for the surviving warriors and for their families.

When I came back to the States from Vietnam, I landed in Fort Lewis, Washington. No protestors greeted me. No one spit at me or anywhere near my direction.

And I don't have any personal knowledge of any veterans who faced such behavior from the public. None ever mentioned it in the circles of vets I knew in college and at a university. And I never heard it from anyone I covered as a newspaper reporter or served as a union representative.

Could it have been one of those urban legends you hear about that lack any real evidence? And what about the "crazed Vietnam veteran" label? I learned through a PTSD clinic that it was hyped up by the press and Hollywood, by well-intentioned liberals seeking to end the Vietnam War. They were in cahoots with activist psychiatrists and psychologists, as well as many others in the medical professions, who were against the war and used the term to scare America into ending it. The problem is the term stayed in the collective consciousness and once again tainted all servicemen, even those who may have served as clerks or cooks in a combat zone or nowhere near the scene of a battle. It got so bad that many veterans refused to add their service record to their résumés, believing it would turn off potential employers.

A study done in the 1970s showed that in most situations when a Vietnam veteran became the subject of the movies or on television, he was generally portrayed as a little deranged at worst or as a loose cannon at best. The term "PTSD," however, had not yet made it into the mainstream. It wasn't until the early 1980s that the bible for mental disorders, the Diagnostic and Statistical Manual of Mental Disorders, first mentioned PTSD and its effects on veterans.

And so I am grateful. They could've called me a lot worse than what they did. But as Contoveros, the "singer of truth" and a daily scrivener here, I hope no one ever calls me "forgetful."

▲   ▲   ▲

On February 2, 2010, at 7:19, my fellow blog-writing friend Steven Goodheart said:

Great post, my friend. As a fellow GI, I appreciate your honesty and insight.

A lot of this stuff was just media hype, and as in all war, there were atrocities. Not that that justifies anything, but it's the sad fact.

Isn't it amazing that it took to the 1980s to recognize PTSD? In World War I, they called it "shell shock" and swept it under the rug.

I love Donovan's song, the "Universal Soldier." It's a *koan* (a riddle to provoke enlightenment) that points to the final answer to war.

On December 23, 2011, at 21:11, Contoveros said:

I listened to the song again, and the words mean so much more while looking back over the years. Thanks so much to Buffy Sainte-Marie for providing us with such loving compassion and understanding in her work of art, the "Universal Soldier."

THE WAR PRAYER

By Mark Twain

O Lord our God, help us tear their soldiers to bloody shreds with our shells; help us to cover their smiling fields with the pale forms of their patriot dead; help us to drown the thunder of the guns with the shrieks of their wounded, writhing in pain; help us to lay waste their humble homes with a hurricane of fire; help us to wring the hearts of their unoffending widows with unavailing grief; help us to turn them out roofless with their little children to wander unfriended in the wastes of their desolated land in rags and hunger and thirst, sports of the sun flames in summer and the icy winds of winter, broken in spirit, worn with travail, imploring thee for the refuge of the grave and denied it—

For our sakes who adore Thee, Lord, blast their hopes, blight their lives, protract their bitter pilgrimage, make heavy their steps, water their way with their tears, strain the white snow with the blood of their wounded feet!
We ask it, in the spirit of love, of Him Who is the Source of Love, and Who is the ever-faithful refuge and friend of all that are sore beset and seek His aid with humble and contrite hearts.

Amen.

GRIEF DELAYED WHILE IN MILITARY SERVICE

https://contoveros.com/2010/04/23/
time-for-grieve-delayed-while-in-the-military/)

I had been in the army less than a week when the news hit me. I had my head shaved; my civilian clothes were exchanged for fatigue pants and a shirt, not to mention boots and headgear, something I had never worn before in my life.

I was drafted on June 3, the day that Billie Joe McAllister jumped off the Tallahatchie Bridge, if I remember the song correctly. I was nineteen years old, knew no one, and was away from my Philadelphia, Pennsylvania, home for first time in 1968.

I quickly learned to fall into formation and step off with the left foot when hearing the command to march. I fell into step with the fellow in front, as well as those to the left and right of me.

I heard some guys talking, violating the sergeant's order not to speak while in formation and while marching. Had to pay attention to the pace being set by the cadence caller announcing in a loud, clear voice to march "to your left...to your left...to your left, right, left" and then answering that same cadence crier who philosophized about loved ones we had just bidden goodbye:

"Ain't no use in going home …

Jody's got your girl and gone.

Sound off."

"One, two."

"Sound off!"

"Three, four…"

Never met anyone named Jody (heard of Jody Powell with President Carter nearly a decade later), but I'd probably not hit it off on meeting someone with that name.

The noise around me continued. More marchers were talking. Louder! Couldn't grasp what was being said at first, but I soon detected the word "dead" being used over and over. Somebody had died. Somebody we all knew. This was June 1968, at Fort Bragg, North Carolina, only a few days after being sworn in as a buck private. And then I experienced one of those moments like when you first heard the Twin Towers were struck or of the assassination of a president decades earlier.

"Bobby Kennedy is dead."

I couldn't grasp the words at first; I didn't want to. Here I was, a soldier, one who had just sworn to uphold the Constitution and do all in my power to protect the country. I couldn't vote. The leadership of the country back then was something I never thought about. Learning the army's business was my only thought and goal.

ᴧ   ᴧ   ᴧ

"Bobby Kennedy is dead."

The words came out again. From someone different this time, someone with a southern accent. The first had a Bronx accent, or maybe one from the heart of New Orleans. They sounded alike to someone exposed to them for the first time. Like me, we were mostly teenagers, hardly any of us near the age of twenty-one.

"Bobby Kennedy is dead." This time I was saying it to myself as I stumbled and wanted desperately to stop playing soldier. I reverted to a one-year-out-of-high-school graduate who had just tasted politics when LBJ bailed out and Bobby entered the presidential race. I liked him. He offered hope to people like me: just off the block, away from the village square, and out from the farmland. For the first time.

▲   ▲   ▲

"Stop!" I wanted to shout. "Stop the marching. Stop the life around me, the pounding, the moving, and the confining. Stop, all of you! Let me be still. Let me pause in the moment. Reflect. Digest.

"For God's sake, please let me grieve."

I needed time to take this in. Someone had shot and silenced perhaps the strongest voice against the Vietnam War and definitely the most influential. Had Bobby Kennedy been elected president, my life may have been different. No memories of firefights, lost comrades, death and destruction...and no PTSD.

Grief, however, eluded me. I was forced to put it off for another day, another place, another life. It was but a foreshadowing of more grief I would encounter before my career ended with the military. It's a grief I am only now dealing with through the practice of meditation and the Omega Institute Retreat on the Cost of War.

But that's another story.

▲   ▲   ▲

(Meanwhile, war, or the threat of one that could lead to nuclear catastrophe, can take its toll on any serviceperson, even if they never set foot into a so-called combat zone. When you're in the military, you are placing yourself in harm's way no matter how far or how near you might believe the enemy is to our doorstep. Take, for instance, my short post in tribute to a young woman named Mary who suffers from post-traumatic stress disorder but can't get anyone at the Veterans Administration to help her overcome her twenty minutes of hell she suffered to safeguard me and you in the early 1980s.)

God and a soldier all people adore in time of war but not before; and when war is over and all things are righted, God is neglected, and an old soldier slighted.

—Anonymous

MARY'S TEARS HELP BATTLE WAR FLASHBACKS

https://contoveros.com/2010/05/03/
marys-tears-help-battle-flashbacks-of-war/

The only thing that seemed to help Mary was the tears.

The act of crying seemed to loosen up and cushion the fear and anxiety that would strike her unexpectedly. Every time she'd hear a siren, she'd feel her chest tighten, her palms sweat, and her heartbeat race.

"Twenty minutes," she'd say and look at a watch or a clock. "It will all be over in twenty minutes."

The world as she knew it would all be over, destroyed by nuclear war.

Mary worked for the North American Air Defense Command (NORAD), serving in the air force, when a glitch of some sort appeared on the computer in the defense system. It was a Friday, when the top brass was either away for a long Veterans Day weekend or not readily available to the skeleton crew left to staff her station. It turns out that twenty-year-old Mary felt responsible for defending the Eastern Seaboard from a nuclear war on November 9, 1979.

It was to strike within twenty minutes, Mary recalled telling a film crew on the grounds of Omega Institute, where she was attending a five-day retreat on what was labeled "The Costs of War" for all veterans with posttraumatic stress, no matter what the situation. That's how much time they believed it would take unless the United States could intercept and/or fire first against the former USSR, the Union of Soviet Socialist Republics.

FULL-SCALE NUCLEAR ATTACK

"I remember leaving my post to go to the bathroom," Mary said. "What I really wanted to do was to call my family. But it would not have done any good."

A full-scale nuclear missile attack on the United States was detected by operators like Mary who were watching display monitors at four major defense sites, including the Pentagon Command Center, according to what is now declassified information.

Instead of using the phone, she returned to her station to deal with the next twenty minutes. (Weeks later, Mary would fall to the floor, crouching into a ball. "Twenty minutes," she'd recall. Twenty minutes until the first bomb would go off. She'd look at her watch. The twenty minutes would pass. No damage to report outside. "Lots of damage inside," Mary would recall.)

Mary rejoined her crew, praying the Our Father with an enlisted man called Evil Dave because of his hard demeanor and a reputation of being the meanest son of a bitch on staff. Mary still recalls how compassionate Evil Dave was that day. They spent long, desperate hours together trying to contact their superiors as NORAD readied for war. During peacetime, the US nuclear arsenal is in a mode known as defense readiness condition, or DEFCON 5. When a threat is perceived, its seriousness determines the level of alert, which can quickly move to the ultimate posture of DEFCON 1, "maximum war readiness."

The state of readiness moved from DEFCON 5 to DEFCON 1. Planes carrying nuclear weapons were launched, as well as the president's jumbo jet housing his nuclear command center, according to published reports. War became imminent. And Mary has not been the same since. She internalized what those exposed to such potential horror experienced. Got physically sick and was hospitalized, only to find out there was little remedy for the stress that occurred when she would hear a siren go off, a loud explosion-like noise, or some other triggering condition that would cause a person to have a PTSD flashback of pain.

But there was no such thing as PTSD. It would not be recognized by mental health experts until years later. No hospital treated anyone with the physical symptoms Mary had expressed. Especially when there was no battle fought.

But Mary battled for years, being forced to leave the air force and seek a home remedy to deal with her nightmares and anxiety attacks. She would simply cry. Crying eased the stress, tension, and fear that often gripped her like a vise. She also exercised. Daily. And spent more and more of her time outdoors with nature.

She still has bouts with the demons from thirty years ago. They became too intense when she was in a PhD program for criminal justice, and she gave it up and ended her PhD program in order to keep her sanity and the peace she obtained by keeping the built-up stress at bay. She found that following a spiritual path helped. A lot. And telling your story so that others might benefit also helps.

The glitch was eventually made public. Mary said there's a movie based on the incident but without all the fancy computer maps. See *WarGames* (1983) and global thermonuclear war. It's based on the experience Mary took part in.

▲ ▲ ▲

ON MAY 4, 2010, AT 05:41, MARY HAMERNICK (THE MARY OF THIS STORY) SAID THE FOLLOWING:

Thanks for the memories! I'm impressed with your memory of the story/history. Here are some clarifications: Evil "Dave" Burnette was a 6′2″, 300-pound African American, and I was a 5′2″, 90-pound White/Irish lass—what a pair.

▲ ▲ ▲

"After realizing the futility of contacting my family, I returned to my post to watch and ready myself for the battle with Evil Dave. It was then, on scope, that I asked him to pray with me, and we did. The crouching and huddling started with the flashbacks and depersonalization which started, with the fury of hell behind them, weeks later."

NOVEMBER 9, 1979

Senator Percy of Florida quotes: "All hell broke loose as 1000 ibcms were spotted incoming from Russia…"

"War, huh, good God. Lord, what is it a good for? Absolutely nothing! Say it again."

ON MAY 4, 2010, AT 08:49, CONTOVEROS SAID:

Thank you, Mary!

I inserted the updates you mention. I am so glad we chatted on that park bench with the cameras rolling in April 2010. We need to tell our stories so other generations might see the futility of war.

—Michael J.

What is absurd and monstrous about war is that men who have no personal quarrel should be trained to murder one another in cold blood.

—Aldous Huxley

WAR GUILT HAUNTS VETERAN YEAR AFTER YEAR

https://contoveros.com/2010/04/23/
war-guilt-haunts-veteran-year-after-year/

I knew something was wrong when I saw the radio operator's face. He handed me the mike attached to the bulky radio strapped on his back. The private, who was new in country, made no eye contact and was hesitant in his actions.

I identified myself by a call sign and heard someone say in a code that the leader of the Third Platoon had just been wounded and that I was ordered to move my First Platoon to give him assistance.

First Lieutenant Victor Lee Ellinger had been shot by the Viet Cong. He was the best of the three platoon leaders in our company, C, of some battalion of the Twenty-Fifth Division. (I can't remember the name of the battalion, which operated near Cu Chi. I block it. I hated the commander, carrying that hate well into my civilian life dozens of years later. He's the only person I know whose own men tried to "frag" him with a hand grenade, but he escaped injury.)

Vic was a college-educated, good-looking Southern boy with a thick head of blond hair and a Southern drawl that got you to like him on first meeting. Had a large, bushy, golden mustache and a swagger about him that signaled "natural-born leader," just like his namesake from his home state of Virginia, Robert E. Lee. Vic hailed from Staunton, Virginia.

He was always on the ball, commanded respect from all his men, and wasn't afraid to raise hell like a drill sergeant when a slacker needed a little extra encouragement to do his duty, even if the task only meant to police the area so the enemy could not find evidence of our movements or, worse yet, set a booby trap to a discarded C ration can or an empty cardboard box that once held four loose cigarettes.

So when I heard Vic was down, I pushed myself harder than I ever did, force-marching my platoon to close the distance to get to him. Not sure how far we marched in the hot jungle, creating our own path with me walking point part of the way in my haste to help.

We got to his position. And we were too late. Vic had died. Two of my men were medevaced out due to heat exhaustion they suffered during the march.

I never did find out the details of his death. We remained in the bush several days until returning to the rear, where we attended a brief ceremony for Vic. My company commander said very little to the remaining two junior officers, even though we—I—had lost one of the closest friends we'd ever have in Vietnam. I never had the time to process Vic's death. I wanted to stop the war then and there. Wanted an answer to the question of why he had to die. What were the circumstances? Why was the platoon leader shot and no one else? Was a sniper with the Viet Cong good enough to take out the guy in charge with such skill?

I wanted to mourn him, to grieve him. I needed to set myself right by him. But I never did. I was ordered back to the field the next day.

Failing to grieve him still haunts me. I have a sense of failure. And when I sink into deep depression, I wish it were me that got killed back then, rather than having to deal with PTSD.

You see, at times, I see Vic as the lucky one. The other platoon leader and I were relieved of our commands after friendly fire episodes. Two Second Platoon grunts that had set out a Claymore mine for an ambush forgot where they put the trip wire and walked into the wire, dying from the explosion almost immediately. Their platoon leader was relieved of his command. I got relieved when I had ordered mortar fire stepped down. "Step down" is an order for the mortar operator to adjust his or her rounds to fall nearer to the target. I wanted the rounds to fall closer to the enemy, and the rounds fell on my own men, injuring half a squad. I carry that guilt with me today.

Good days and bad days. Meditation and bringing dark war wounds out to the light helps to ease the pain.

So does Omega Institute and programs like Buddhist Monk and former Vietnam War machine gunner Claude AnShin Thomas's retreat, called "The Cost of War."

You can have all the advanced war methods you want, but, after all, nobody has ever invented a war that you don't have to have somebody in the guise of soldiers to stop the bullets.

—Will Rogers

LIGHT SHINES FROM A
TIP OF THE CANDLE

https://contoveros.com/2010/04/27/
light-shines-here-from-a-tip-of-the-candle/amp/

Veterans are the light at the tip of the candle, illuminating the way for the whole nation. If veterans can achieve awareness, transformation, understanding, and peace, they can share with the rest of society the realities of war.

And they can teach us how to make peace with ourselves and each other, so we never have to use violence to resolve conflicts again.

—Thich Nhat Hanh, Vietnamese Buddhist monk

It's funny how those who are most pro-war are almost always the guys who never had to fight in one.

—Jerome P. Crabb

GOING AWOL HELPS BOY GROW TO A MAN

https://contoveros.com/2010/09/21/
going-awol-helps-a-boy-grow-into-a-man/

I went AWOL while serving as a private in the US Army in 1968.
I had finished my basic training at Fort Bragg, North Carolina, and remained there an additional three long months, serving as a glorified "gofer" in a battalion commander's office while awaiting a "secret clearance" to be completed. I had been away from home for no more than a few days prior to that. And when at nineteen I found myself transferred from the Deep South back north to New Jersey, I skipped out of Fort Dix by going AWOL to my home in Philadelphia.

I didn't see myself as being away without official leave. I arrived on a Friday and did not have to report for Advanced Individual Training until that Monday, and using my inborn initiative, I left the barracks and made my way to a bus station and then home.

My father had been mugged while I was away those past five months. He ended up in the hospital, and the assault probably caused his health to decline, forcing him to stop working at the age of sixty-nine. (Or was it seventy-one? You couldn't tell with Pop. Achilles Contoveros lied about his age. Federal records show two different dates of birth for him. One was probably offered by him under an alias when incarcerated for bootlegging in New York City.)

My family was in the process of moving from Brewerytown to Wayne, Pennsylvania, a section of Philadelphia's Main Line called "Little Chicago." I liked their new digs and saw the house briefly after finishing Advanced Individual Training and serving as an acting corporal at a training camp later. But I had but one stripe on my arm when I visited in late November. Heck, I had sewed the stripe on myself with needle and thread in a barracks where I lived without a radio, television, or another soul for what seemed forever.

I went cold turkey when I was drafted on June 3, 1968. Life as I knew it came to an end, as I got word of an outside world only by way of mouth. The first two months really didn't matter. A mean and nasty drill sergeant had given me no time for anything but army life, and he took pleasure in ordering additional push-ups for privates like me planning to attend Officer Candidate School. That's why I needed the secret clearance. It's required of anyone seeking to become a military leader and possibly deal with sensitive government details.

Going to OCS was my older brother's idea. George Stanley Contos was what we called a lifer, one who'd spend at least twenty years in the military, thereby insuring a pension the rest of his life, plus PX, or "post exchange," privileges and other benefits. As a sergeant, he learned I scored well on leadership tests (don't know how; I barely made it through high school, where I majored in lunch). He insisted I become an officer, believing military life would be better for me as a lieutenant than as a noncommissioned officer. I ended up leading a combat infantry platoon in Vietnam and got PTSD as a result of it later.

Thanks a lot, brother!

I got into a fight at Thirtieth and Poplar Streets in North Philadelphia during my visit home. You see, I wore my uniform, and some street toughs wanted a piece of the "soldier boy." One of them threw something at me outside of Merschen's Bar, and I retaliated by grabbing a metal trash can lid and charging at them gladiator-style. We exchanged words, not blows, and went our separate ways, with me upholding the reputation as one of our country's soon-to-be blossoming killing machines.

As I returned to Fort Dix, I remembered hearing the Beatles' "Hey Jude" played over the radio for the first time. I wanted to cry. It was being introduced as an oldie, I thought, and I wanted to know where my life as a child had gone, how I had found myself on the threshold of becoming a man. I missed my home, my friends, and my old girlfriend. I'd lose all of them over the three years I'd serve in the army. I'd be forced to grow up more quickly by becoming an officer and leading boys only slightly younger than myself in combat less than two years later.

After accidentally going AWOL, I got off with just a warning when the company commander, a captain, called me into his office on my return. I explained my story in detail to him. He appreciated my candor and declined to issue an Article 15, a nonjudicial punishment that would have prevented me from entering OCS. I learned there comes a time when a person has to put away their childish ways and see the world as an adult. I did back then, but I kept the memory of that child to let him loose now and then to tell a story or two. I gotta make sure, however, he doesn't go AWOL on me.

War would end if the dead could return.

—Stanley Baldwin

INTERLUDE: "ABRAHAM, MARTIN AND JOHN" LIVE ON

https://contoveros.com/2010/08/29/
abraham-martin-john-live-on-within/

Rain pours on me while I am outside on guard duty in the afternoon hours sometime late in 1968. But soft music warms and shelters me on the inside. "Abraham, Martin and John," the song, plays from this relatively new gadget (created just 19 years earlier) that is a portable, hand-held transistor radio.

I'm on guard duty as a buck private, having been in the US Army six months now. I'm wearing a slick poncho, an "OD" green-colored sheet of material that's like a rubber covering that got mixed with a substance created just a decade earlier, something called "plastic." The poncho is yucky. Gives me the creeps. (I'll refuse to wear it again during my three-year military stint. Even in the rainy seasons in Vietnam and Panama, I'll let my clothes get soaking wet and allow them to dry rather than permit the poncho's snakelike feel on my bare skin.)

On this day in Fort Dix, New Jersey, however, I wear a "steel-pot" helmet and carry an M14 rifle beneath the poncho. I've just ducked into a makeshift tent when the rain starts to fall really hard. It keeps pouring, and there is nothing for me to do but stare out into the torrential downpour and let my mind drift…

As well as turn on the radio…

And hear Dion DiMucci, formerly of Dion and the Belmonts, sing a mournful song that was more gospel-sounding than his usual teenage rock and roll efforts of "Teenager in Love" and "I Wonder Why," not to mention "The Wanderer" and "Donna the Prima Donna."

He's singing of men who gave their lives for their country and their beliefs. Persons who placed their ideals above corporeal comfort. All shot down. All killed. And all growing so much larger in the wake of their assassinations.

Didn't you love…the things that they stood for?
Didn't they try…to find some good…for you…and me?

It's taken me the entire length of the song to realize who Dion is actually singing about. John F. Kennedy and Martin Luther King come easy. But I get stuck on Abraham. (And this morning, some forty years later, I got stuck again when the phrase from that song came to me: "Is anybody wondering?" Abraham arises in my mind: Abraham of the Bible, the Old Testament, and the father of our world's three major religions, Judaism, Islam, and Christianity. I began to "wonder" whether the song is supposed to stretch back to that old man. The one with a long white beard who's prepared to kill his son—what was his name? Isaac?—and, in performing such a sacrifice, pass a test imposed by the Lord.)

No way can I linger with this thought, so I switch and focus on another relatively young bearded man named Abraham. Abraham Lincoln, whose wife, Mary Todd Lincoln, convinced her husband to host a spiritualist medium to conduct the first séance at the White House. It is that Abraham the song addresses.

Anybody here seen my old friend Abraham?
Can you tell me where he's gone?
He freed a lot of people,
But it seems the good, they die young.
You know, I just looked around, and he's gone.

The song laments the death of two presidents and a great civil rights champion and then poses a question that only came about because of tragedy occurring six months earlier to another Kennedy.

Anybody here seen my old friend Bobby?
I thought I saw him walkin' up over the hill
With Abraham, Martin and John.

The rain eventually stops. So does guard duty. But the song's message continues on through this day: "Find some good for you and me…"

All the war-propaganda, all the screaming and lies and hatred, comes invariably from people who are not fighting.

—George Orwell

NEVER ASK 'EM TO DO
WHAT YOU WOULDN'T DO

Walking meditation as taught in the Buddhist tradition reminds me a lot of how we used to walk in Vietnam, particularly in thick jungle areas. We'd go slowly, step by cautious step, remaining keenly aware of our surroundings and vigilant of the present moment. I focused on the next spot on the ground where I'd place my foot and the path up ahead as far as I could see. I wouldn't think of anything as I held the M16 across my chest at the ready point in case I needed to fire quickly. I'd be on high alert, letting my senses take in anything that seemed the least bit harmful or threatening.

We never exploded enemy mines or booby traps by accidentally walking on them. We were lucky. I never heard of anyone in our battalion that triggered any. Years later I met a fellow from my Catholic grade school drafted two years before my time who was not so fortunate. Pete walked on a mine and spent the rest of his life dealing with the impairment. Several doctors wanted to remove the more damaged leg, but he wouldn't let them cut him. He was right and, with the assistance of a cane, has walked on his own, feeling fortunate nothing worse had occurred.

More recently, I met a veteran who actually did lose a leg. Some enemy soldier, Viet Cong I suppose, tossed a hand grenade in his direction. He told a group of vets he had only two choices: getting up and running away or staying still. He remained still, and the explosion ripped off one of his appendages. Had he gotten up to flee, the whole left side of his body would have blown away. He counted himself as lucky to have lived, sans one of his legs. Being impaired did not prevent him from such careers as later working in the US Post Office, as an administrator for the Veterans Administration, and as a teacher.

I walked point on some occasions. I never asked someone to do something I wouldn't do, except perhaps to carry an M60, the largest weapon a squad would haul while on patrol. The biggest guy usually got that assignment, and at five foot, six inches and 140 pounds, I would never have fit the bill. I'd cut through overgrown jungle with a machete, giving a Vietnamese Kit Carson scout a break from that routine. ("Kit Carson" was the name we gave to the Vietnamese regulars assigned as scouts for each platoon. Carson was a famous scout who aided the US Army in the opening of the Old West in the latter part of the nineteenth century.) You don't know how tiring it can get, whack after whack, moving ever so slowly through paths that didn't exist until someone cut a new one.

One of the most peaceful moments of my life occurred in Vietnam. We were on a routine mission when we came across a humongous crater in the ground. The crater was twenty feet deep with a diameter of about forty feet. Vegetation was growing throughout the hole as well as the bank where we pulled up and eventually set up a makeshift camp during the daylight hours. The first thing I noticed was the absence of noise. The only sounds were natural ones that seemed clearer or more amplified somehow by the configuration of the area. Birds made sounds in harmony with insects that played a symphony of notes and vibrations.

I lost any and all fear I might have had up to that moment. Concerns and worries melted away. We sat at the top of that crater and rested in such a calm and peaceful moment, it felt uncanny. Before that moment, I had never felt so insulated and protected from the cares of the outside world. I had never felt it before and only rarely ever since. Had there been a temple here before we arrived? Was this holy land we had accidentally trespassed upon?

No. It turns out the spot was on the outskirts of a rubber tree plantation. But we didn't know that until we stayed the night and decamped the next day, our low-energy batteries recharged and our hearts and minds uplifted with a clearer and stronger resolve.

I felt like someone mysteriously had massaged parts of my psyche that were sore and beaten from humping in the boonies day after day with no reprieve except a three-day visit to a rear camp every two weeks. We ate nothing but canned food called C rations and took no baths or showers. A good-sized tree off in the distance was what we used to relieve ourselves for fourteen days in a row. Use deodorant? Forget it. Bug spray? After three or four days in the jungle, all Vietnamese bugs got sick and tired of the taste of Americans, preferring the carcass of some animal long dead. It probably smelled better than we did.

Moving away from the crater, we saw a plantation building not more than two hundred yards away. There it was: a two-story mansion right smack-dab in the middle of the jungle. It had balconies and columns around doorways and windows and reminded me more of a New Orleans country home than some Saigon-area dwelling. We learned the French had built it and used it as part of some operations with the rubber trees nearby. There was an adjoining tennis court and an Olympic-sized swimming pool next to that. Years later I'd joke on how I ordered a machine gunner to secure the far end of the empty pool while placing a fire team at the nearer side of the tennis court.

Accompanied by my radio operator and two other soldiers, we marched to the front door, knocked, and entered when greeted by Vietnamese civilians working inside. Upon entering one room, I saw the longest mahogany bar I had ever seen stretched out for what seemed like forever. It could have easily handled one hundred people sipping Irish whiskey while munching cashews.

I walked toward the bar feeling very much like John Wayne as I placed my M16 on the magnificently polished wood. I ordered a round of sodas, got something that resembled a bad-tasting cola, and offered to pay for it with military scrip, which was politely refused. Hours later I squatted in a tiny room with members of the Vietnamese family that took care of the building and grounds. There were lots of children and lots of lentil-like soup passed around. I never got more details. We spent the night and moved on without telling my company commander the real reason why we had remained in that area. I looked at this little interlude as an R & R from the firefights we had recently been engaged in.

You can discover peace in the dead center of a war, if you know how to seek it.

⅄ ⅄ ⅄

I would recall that day in the jungle years later when I had taken part in a twenty-one-day meditation retreat via the internet. I joined an online meditation offered by Deepak Chopra and Oprah Winfrey.

It was August 22, 2014, the anniversary of my commission as an officer in the US Army, and I took the occasion to remember one of the most peaceful moments of my life.

It turned out that the greatest sense of peace I have ever felt had occurred while I was in the middle of a war.

It's sort of funny how God can work in mysterious ways, isn't it? The next story deals with one of question posed by Deepak at a twenty-one-day meditation program and the answer I wrote for the blog Contoveros.WordPress.com.

If you wish to be brothers, drop your weapons.

—Pope John Paul II

PEACE FOUND IN THE MIDDLE OF VIETNAM WAR

https://contoveros.com/2014/08/22/
peace-found-inside-middle-of-vietnam-war/)

Recall a time when you felt calm and peaceful, even though the circumstances were not peaceful. Write down a description of that event and describe how you were able to be calm in that situation. What was the source of this peacefulness if it didn't come from outside?

—Deepak Chopra, 21-Day Meditation
Experience (Day Three, "Feeling Peace")

I had led my platoon in Vietnam for several months. We had encountered several firefights, but no one was killed or injured, thank God. But you never knew what the next day would bring, so we were on edge, at the ready, so to speak, for anything that might have endangered us.

And then one day, I led one of my two squads into an area where we came across a humongous crater that had been carved in the earth. I don't know what kind of bomb had created such a massive hole. It looked as if it had been there for several years before the ten or twelve guys that I was leading approached it. Circling it, we decided to make our overnight camp there.

▲　▲　▲

It was broad daylight, however, when we got to it, and there were still several hours of light left. I'll tell you: I have never felt so much peace as I did when settling in at that moment. I don't know what it was that gave off such calm and relaxing vibrations. Perhaps there had been a monastery or some sort of temple there at one time. Perhaps spirits from those prayers offered up to whatever gods existed at their time were still lingering in the vicinity.

I felt secure and comfortable. I felt I could rest and not worry of any type of attack, even though we didn't let down our watch through the evening or overnight. It just seemed as if God had gathered us in His arms and was protecting us.

I hadn't felt that presence of God since I was twelve years old. I didn't recognize it as a presence until recently, when I reflected on the more peaceful times in my life and determined that, strangely enough, they were right smack in the middle of a war.

The peace came from within but also from the birds and critters that had returned to what must have been a burned-out shell shortly after the massive explosion. Bushes and small trees had started to grow along the sides of the crater. There weren't that many flowers, but the foliage was pleasant to look at, and I was comforted to believe it could conceal us from outside forces. Maybe it did.

And maybe that is what peace is all about: being able to go within, protected from outside forces.

PART II

Focusing on the worst day of your life assumes a great deal. The first is that you believe that nothing could compare to one day in your entire life that was more horrendous than any other day, including any and all days of your future life.

But I believe that I have seen the worst happen. Nothing that I can imagine could possibly compare. (Knock on wood!) There were so many emotions that erupted all at once. None really ever got processed or was allowed to surface in broad daylight. I kept them underneath the surface until they bullied their way from those dark recesses inside to get into my mind and capture it years later.

Unlike many veterans injured in war, I received no visible wounds. Mine were of the psychological type. I didn't know their severity until they took over, flashing their sense of fear and rage in current-day activities, making me a prisoner to the past. I couldn't shake them in stressful situations, and now that I better understand their effect on me, I must try to keep my mind on more wholesome things like love and compassion that I find through meditation and acts of kindness for others.

I must stop waging war inside of myself and continually seek the peace I know is at the center of my being.

It is not enough to say we must not wage war. It is necessary to love peace and sacrifice for it.

—Martin Luther King, Jr.

LIFE SPAN OF SECOND LIEUTENANT— SIXTEEN MINUTES

Cu Chi, South Vietnam, November of 1970

I halted the platoon's movement before we got to the river's edge. I couldn't shake the feeling of uncertainty and fear of a possible ambush at the crossing. There may have been a residual effect from the shelling we took the day before. It might have colored my thinking.

Or maybe I was just afraid.

There, I said it. How many years has it taken me to admit something I never wanted to look at, let alone possibly admit? Looking back, I have finally realized that it is not unmanly or uncourageous to say that I feared for myself and for my men. I was afraid of what might lie across the fifty-foot river. I had not felt this way since coming across that invisible sniper who gained my respect, forcing me to seek a different path rather than go full steam ahead to wherever he had taken up a position. I will deal with that episode in my life later on in this book.

That sniper who fired upon me and the squad I was leading a few weeks earlier could have been in a tree, behind a bush, or in any direction to our front at the left or the right. We got to the hill along a different route with no one shot.

I moved the men forward but got fired at by that sniper repeatedly. I didn't know where the next well-aimed bullet might strike. It struck the spot where I had slowly offered to take a step. Pieces of rock, soil, and foliage spat at me, part of a ricochet disturbance the sniper's bullet caused. It forced me to rethink my purpose in Vietnam. My mission was to get from point A to point B and to not get myself or any of my troops killed in some stupid act of bravado. Let the sniper be. You'd lose too much to try to get him. Just report his position to higher-ups. They could decide whether it was worth storming up a hill. They could bring in a ranger team, a few of whom even trained as snipers and knew the best way, if any, to flush him out.

Don't forget what happened to Lt. Vic Ellinger, the Third Platoon leader. He could have been hired by central casting for the job of combat infantry leader. He wasn't especially tall, but he had a charisma that mixed well with his Southern accent. He reminded me of General George Custer, hell-bent leader of the Seventh Army Calvary that Sitting Bull and Crazy Horse defeated at the Battle of the Little Bighorn.

This was younger Custer, at least one that my mind created as to what he must have looked like. A blond-haired Errol Flynn or a Peter O'Toole, but without the flowing white robes of a Lawrence of Arabia. Vic had a no-non-sense leadership approach and had a lot of street sense for a fellow from Virginia. There was a swagger about him. A certain charisma that made you want to listen to and follow him just for the hell of it. You knew he'd accomplish the mission while looking out for the welfare of the men, and you wanted to be part of that experience.

A sniper shot Vic to death. He was the only member of the Third Platoon to take fire while walking into an ambush. No one else got hit. No one except for the platoon leader had been singled out. No one else died. How good this enemy soldier must have been to focus solely on, and take out, the leader.

There used to be some urban legend about the amount of time some officers ended up serving in Vietnam.

"What's the life span of a second lieutenant in Vietnam?"

"Sixteen minutes," they would say.

I never thought about it while in Vietnam. I never looked at myself as a marked man. But I guess I was—marked, that is. Maybe marked not only by the Viet Cong but in some rare circumstances by our own troops. You might get marked if you ran things by the book and didn't listen to the advice of the noncommissioned officers and combat-tested veterans who knew not only how to fight but, just as importantly, if not more, how to stay alive. American troops have been known to shoot their own leaders. In all the cases that I have heard of, it usually involved an officer who through ignorance recklessly endangered the lives of himself and men around him. Usually it was an inexperienced young man who would have earned his commission through West Point, Officer Candidate School, or through Reserve Officers' Training Corps. Battlefield commissions also catapulted a soldier to the officers' ranks, but I never heard of any seasoned man who foolishly exposed his men to danger, thereby attracting such a desperate act.

Second lieutenants were not the only targets of such retribution. My battalion commander, Lt. Col. Ralph Salucci, was fired on by his own troops. At least one soldier tried to kill or seriously injure him while "fragging" the colonel's bunker. Sandbags placed strategically around the bunker prevented any injury while the officer slept inside, but word of the attempt spread throughout the encampment. There were several grunts in my company that would have not been saddened a bit had the hand grenade accomplished its mission. I counted myself among them before and after he had relieved me of my command following a friendly fire incident.

One of my brother's brothers-in-law was rumored to have been dishonorably discharged from the military after he allegedly fired on an officer. I don't know the details, but I believe the officer was new in country and had not been acclimatized to Vietnam by a good platoon sergeant. Perhaps the combat infantryman felt justified in trying to look out for his well-being and the well-being of others. But what a way to end your military career, not to mention the lieutenant whose life would have ended if the private were a better shot.

Our reason for being in Vietnam was never clear to me. All most of us knew was that we were there to help the people of South Vietnam against the enemy from North Vietnam, the so-called regulars (North Vietnam?), and the Viet Cong, who mingled with the villages and often employed civilians to battle the American soldier. We were to fight the "enemy," some vague concept of a people that were either the enemy of the United States or what turned out to be the corrupt and repressive government of South Vietnam.

Killing is killing, no matter what side unleashes the firepower. You have to believe your country is morally right in taking such action. There comes a time, however, when you realize people on the other side have as much faith, if not more, in their own beliefs to take up arms against others. It made no sense to me years after the war, and I guess there were few if any wars that made a lot of sense in any period of time.

I destroy my enemies when I make them my friends.

—Abraham Lincoln

FROM ASSORTED
BOXES OF C RATIONS

"Shit" detail for those in Vietnam was literally just that: detail for a soldier, usually a buck private, to burn feces that gathered in the bottom of latrines. A good soldier learned to stir the shit while it burned in order to accomplish a mission of health and safety. You wouldn't want anyone getting injured from anything but an AK-47.

The first time that I ever saw the word "fuck" or its derivative in an American mainstream journal was in *Time* magazine when an article referred to the "REMFs" who served in Vietnam. The acronym was for the soldiers who did not serve in direct combat or contact with the enemy but in a support role from a base camp or some secured area in what World War I military men called the "rear." Troops fighting in trenches were fighting in the "front lines."

Grunts who humped the bush—that is, engaged the enemy on patrols and through reconnaissance missions in the "field"—called those soldiers working in the rear "REMFs": "Rear Echelon Motherfuckers." That's according to *Time* magazine.

We would go fourteen days without bathing while in the bush. I stopped wearing underwear after learning it took so much longer for it to dry during the rainy season and while walking through a river or a stream. (We simply wanted to avoid something called "crotch rot.")

I continued this about two years after getting back to civilian life, never wearing briefs or boxer shorts beneath my pants, even when I'd wear a suit. There are some days even today that I miss the certain freedom it offered.

▲   ▲   ▲

I didn't worry about grooming myself that much. I don't think I combed my hair much or shaved, even though I might have had a razor in my backpack. Who was there to look good for? Some mama-san or baby-san you'd see in a village?

▲   ▲   ▲

I didn't brush my teeth. I got used to morning breath. By taking that early morning breath of air, at least I knew I had survived one more day to take another breath.

▲   ▲   ▲

Leeches never discriminated by rank when we'd walk through waters where they'd congregate. They'd bite you whether you were a commissioned or a noncommissioned officer or a buck private new in country.

None ever got through my boots, but the leeches loved my back as well as the thighs and spots just below my private area. You couldn't get rid of all of them by yourself, and you had to trust someone with steady hands to burn the ones sucking at your back.

I never want to ever see a leech again. Once bitten, you would know why.

▲   ▲   ▲

Soldiers learned quickly to never crap alone in the wooded areas we walked from sunup to sundown. You always staked out a secluded spot with a buddy who would keep an eye out and an M16 pointed to ensure no one surprised you in such a vulnerable position while squatting.

And though I've tried, I can't recall one time at all that I took care of this routine business. I guess nothing out of the ordinary had ever occurred, so I blocked all memories of deposits left in the jungle.

⋏   ⋏   ⋏

While in Vietnam, we used the military phonetic code whenever we spoke over the radio. It helped you spell out words while speaking over the "horn." It followed the regular alphabet and consisted of the following:

ALPHA	A
BRAVO	B
CHARLIE	C
DELTA	D
ECHO	E
FOXTROT	F
GULF	G
HOTEL	H
INDIA	I
JULIET	J
KILO	K
LIMA	L
MIKE	M
NOVEMBER	N
OSCAR	O
PAPA	P
ROMEO	R
SIERRA	S

TANGO	T
UNIFORM	U
VICTOR	V
WHISKEY	W
X-RAY	X
YANKEE	Y
ZULU	Z

"Over and Out!"

Make the lie big, make it simple, keep saying it, and eventually they will believe it.

—Adolph Hitler

MY UNOFFICIAL
VIEW OF PTSD

Posttraumatic stress occurs when a person undergoing a traumatic experience is unable or not allowed the time to process the explosion of something horrific or extremely startling to the psyche, to their very being. At least that's my interpretation from the years of therapy I've undergone for anger management and later the more properly diagnosed PTSD.

Thoughts of a career, a family, a house, and a car take over, outweighing the need to focus on the past. You can think about the horror later, not now, when a promotion or a dinner with an influential businessperson can make or break your move up the corporate ladder, your "in" with the boss, or the deal that needs a skillful "you" to usher it through to fruition.

Let's not forget a brand-new car for your spouse. You promised them that the next new car purchase would be for their use. Keep an eye out for a "beater," an older car, to give your teenager to work on while driving it upon graduation from high school. What about remodeling the kitchen or the bathroom or making that addition to the house that you had always talked about?

Posttrauma issues? Who's got time for those? Don't need to deal with them now. "If it ain't broke, don't fix it," my former labor union boss used to tell me.

But then some things start to feel broken; they feel frayed or about to tear apart when, up until that point, everything had seemed to hold together so nicely. You feel you don't have the same control you did over certain situations. You could handle just about anything over the past twenty to twenty-five years. You'd pull all-nighters and appear fresh the next day for another round of work and life's challenges. Multiple tasking was a cinch, one series of stress-inducing incidents after another.

Cracks start forming across the shell of your demeanor, though. You notice that you yell more. You yell more loudly. More things irritate you. They're little things that were annoyances but now seem so aggravating. You don't have patience for them anymore.

I used to curse them silently and then more openly, giving voice to some latent pain that surfaced from somewhere deep inside. Soon I began cursing at a supermarket clerk while standing in line, impatiently calculating the loss of time she'd cause with her slow service and demanding to see her manager to blow out of proportion whatever the matter was that set me off at the start.

My wrath wasn't just reserved for strangers doing what I perceived to be some disservice to me. Why couldn't my spouse see the many frustrations life had been dealing me lately? Couldn't she see the intolerable conditions that anyone facing what I was facing would fall prey to? I wanted to overcome the stress certain encounters brought with them. I wanted to destroy the causes that led to the attacks on me. The last time I felt these almost indescribable feelings was when the original trauma first hit: the missile explosion, the blasting away of a body part, the death of a soldier by a sniper's bullet.

Trauma erupted, jarring my body and mind, but it was pushed aside, forced into a part of me that would deal with it later as my survival training and military-shaped reflexes kicked in and I focused on actions needed immediately. I could process these earth-shattering encounters later, when it was safer, when I had the time, when the present moment didn't need my absolutely clear focus and deep concentration.

That time never came, did it? The trauma was never sorted out. It would never disappear but instead percolate far beneath the surface of my daily life, almost as if waiting for more and more stress to fill its vessel to the brim, when it would have no choice but to erupt like boiling water too hot for my coolheaded self to contain anymore.

Whoa! What's going on in my world? Why are these feelings cropping up now after I had things so much under control all of these years?

At least I thought I had them under control.

It's the unprocessed stuff that never saw the light of day, Michael J.: all that crap you put behind you and that stiff upper lip of dealing with it "as a man," telling yourself, "You can take it, my boy. Put it all behind you and go on to the next challenge, the next fight, the next…whatever."

But you're not the same young man that could take a licking and keep on ticking. Today's licking knocks you on your ass, and it's harder to get back up. Your heart beats fast. Your heart beats louder, one long thump after another, as if you had just run a mile in six minutes or experienced a shock to your system, causing you to become dry-mouthed and your palms to sweat. All of a sudden, you ain't there anymore. You're back to a time when the trauma first slapped you upside your head and went unprocessed underground. Your body is demanding you deal with the trauma now, this very moment, as a present-day stressor triggers those buried memories.

Some of the best treatments for posttraumatic stress suggest that a person should relive those terrifying moments. Reexperiencing a bombing, a shooting, or an assault (or the experiencing of witnessing any or all of the above) can serve as medicine under proper supervision and guidance. When done under the right conditions, you can unlock feelings and emotions stored away decades earlier. Some of us cry. I cried uncontrollably for short periods of time.

"To hell with ideas of 'manliness,'" I said to no one in particular.

I watched men get wounded, helped to bury a fellow officer, and saw men turn to alcohol and drugs before ever leaving the zone of combat. We all took the war back home with us in order to deal with it the best way we could.

It wasn't my fault they got injured. I did not cause the circumstances leading to their deaths. I'm not to blame. And if you made it out, too, neither are you. No, those who didn't return turned out to be the lucky ones. We who survived carry with us demons that only the savagery of war can create and cause to linger until a time when its brutal ugliness resurfaces years later.

All the wrong people remember Vietnam. I think all the people who remember it should forget it, and all the people who forgot it should remember it.

—Michael Herr

PTSD WOUNDS BUT LEAVES NO VISIBLE SCARS

My journey to try to make some sense out of Vietnam and its effect on me started in 2008, when I was diagnosed with posttraumatic stress disorder and psychologists determined it was so chronic that it caused permanent disability. I obtained counseling from Howard Cohen, PsyD, recommended by a veteran who suggested I go to the Veterans Administration because we suffered from similar physical problems.

Both of us were denied for our recurring stomach problems, but we learned that many veterans were facing the same things we had been experiencing: nightmares, anxieties with new situations, rage, hyperawareness, and flashbacks.

The flashbacks got so bad that I got into three fights with assistant district attorneys in the last two months I served as a public defender in Philadelphia. I felt angry all of the time and lashed out at people, usually hurting myself more than anyone else.

FLASHBACKS CAUSE EMOTIONAL STRESS TODAY

What's a flashback? It is an emotional response to a situation that triggers a memory of something horrendous that has happened in a person's past. Not only do you experience the emotional response you had before but your body has a physical response. I would begin to sweat. My palms sweated.

My throat would also get very dry. My heart rate would increase to a point where I thought my heart was going to burst.

And I was at the ready to immediately attack!

I fought back, attacking what I thought was the threat at that very moment, never realizing that the only threat I ever faced was in my mind.

▲ ▲ ▲

Let me give you an example. I represented a young woman who was a heroin addict. She was charged with attempted murder, and an assistant district attorney from the highly trained "habitual offenders" office was assigned to prosecute the twenty-five-year-old white woman.

What was her offense? She was accused of trying to infect the manager of a Rite Aid store with hepatitis B by sticking him with a tainted needle she had pulled from her pocket. My client had tested positive for hepatitis B when tested upon her arrest and placement in prison. The DA's office claimed she tried to kill the store manager with the needle while resisting arrest for the crime of retail theft.

Yeah, she was shoplifting. She had a long record of shoplifting and drug possession. Nothing more. In other words, she was a junkie who stole from stores to help support her habit.

On the day she was arrested, she had placed deodorant and toothpaste, among other things, into her jacket pockets. She made an unwise decision, you see. She had gone into the same Rite Aid she had stolen things from about a year earlier. The store manager and one of the employees recognized her and watched her walk through the aisles of the store and take the items.

The manager approached her and asked her to stop. She made a movement to get away from him, and the employee grabbed her hair from behind and pulled it. My client had her hands in her pockets, and she pulled them out to balance herself and turned toward the clerk behind her.

She poked herself with the needle in one of her pockets. It got stuck, and the needle came out of the pocket as the toothpaste fell to the floor. The needle twisted and came undone from where it had stuck her at the base of her right thumb. It was in her hand, however, when she swung her arm backward and in the direction of the unseen assailant who had just yanked her hair.

In court, the clerk testified that she tried to stab him. Because of the positive hepatitis test, my client was charged with trying to murder him.

When she told me her story, she said that the test done at the hospital was a false positive and that the doctor who had treated her earlier could verify that.

I was in the process of gathering that evidence to present it the assistant district attorney. The prosecutor made an offer of five to ten years in prison in return for a guilty plea. I had hoped to negotiate less time in return for a plea. So I told the state's representative about what my client had said.

"Well, when did she learn it was false positive?" the prosecutor asked. "She might have not known that at the time of the incident."

I went berserk while in the courtroom where we had been discussing the case. I flipped out and cursed out that assistant DA, telling her to get the fuck out of the courtroom. My client had just been brought to the defense table in handcuffs, and I didn't want this DA representative to be in a position to possibly eavesdrop on what I had discussed with the defendant.

I saw red and wanted to hurt the prosecutor. I flashed back to the time in Vietnam when my actions led to my own men's being injured through my mistake: "It was my fault back then. It's my fault now."

I left the Defender Association shortly after this incident, and I never looked back on what happened with the defendant. I felt ashamed and guilty, just like I'd felt some forty years earlier.

That is what "post-traumatic" actually means: the trauma reoccurs after the event. Things in our daily life could trigger the emotional recall, and in many cases, the trauma prevents a normal person from living a normal life.

Thanks to a veteran I met in court, I learned that I was not alone. I got help and continue to deal with the devils from my past through meditation, counseling, and prayer.

⋏　⋏　⋏

PTSD leaves no physical wounds, no physical deformities or physical scars. But it causes wounds that never seem to heal. And that was the moral for the following story, the first article I ever wrote about PTSD for the Contoveros blog at Contoveros.Wordpress.com.

SOME WOUNDS
NEVER HEAL—JUST
ASK PHILLY JOE

https://contoveros.com/2009/10/15/some-wounds-never-heal/

War changed Joe.
It stripped him of all interest in leading people in any official capacity. Forever.

He has never been the same since coming home, but he didn't know that until years later, when he was shaken awake to this harsh reality through a PTSD session on Vietnam.

They called Joe "Philly" in the US Army squad he commanded. The City of Brotherly Love was his home, and many, like him, took on the name of their state or city while in the service. He was a sergeant, in charge of a squad of grunts, infantry soldiers who canvassed the bush, the jungle of Vietnam, helicopter flight after helicopter flight.

Joe was the type of leader that men loved to serve with—honest and compassionate yet firm, with a no-nonsense approach when a crisis called for it. More importantly, Joe's men followed him because each knew from experience that Joe would not ask you to do anything that he would not have done himself.

That's why Harris, a young recruit who heard of Joe's military savvy, had asked to become a member of his squad, his "fire team."

"I made him my machine gunner," Joe recalled. In addition to carrying the heavy weapon, Harris packed a .45 pistol, a weapon generally handled by those not carrying an M16.

And it happened one day that Harris had quietly approached Joe and told the sergeant he had lost the handgun. The squad was flown in by helicopter to a section where all dismounted and slowly spread out, marching nearly a half a klick (half a kilometer, or five hundred meters) before Harris discovered the loss and approached the sarge, confiding in him.

Joe did not want Harris to get into trouble for losing the military-issued weapon. More importantly, Joe said, he did not want the enemy to get their hands on it and use it against some GI.

So Joe ordered his squad to stand down and wait as he and Harris made their way back through an untrodden path, making their way back to the landing zone.

They found the gun!

And the Viet Cong found them!

Joe and Harris came under fire, being shot from some small arms from some unknown direction. They moved quickly, trying to retrace their steps away from the now marked area and get to the safety of the other men.

An unseen enemy sharpshooter, who had apparently lain in wait for the Americans, hit Harris. Joe saw Harris take the shot, and the sergeant propped up the "younger man." (Joe was all of eighteen years old when he directed the lives of the "kids," those who were new in country.) Harris struggled, but with Joe's help, both made it back to safety.

"You got a million-dollar wound," Joe remembered telling Harris as he helped to attend to his single wound. "You're going home," he added, trying his best to keep the injured soldier calm and relaxed, focused on something other than the pain that could too easily force him to go into shock. It worked. The young man's injuries appeared to stabilize when a helicopter crew flew in to medevac him out of the field and to an army hospital...

Where Harris died from his wound.

Thus injuring a major part of Joe's psyche. Joe's soul. And his outlook on the rest of his life.

Oh, Joe finished his tour just fine, getting out of the war zone one month short of a twelve-month rotation. But he never felt the same way as he did in giving orders before the loss of Harris.

It haunted him in a way he only recently realized. You see, Joe has never sought advancement in any of the jobs or career paths he chose after the war.

"They wanted me to be a supervisor," Joe said of assembly-line work he once produced in a factory. Joe turned the position down cold.

Years later, while serving as a correctional officer in the prison system, Joe smiled and simply refused to follow the advice of others urging him to "put in" for sergeant. The same thing occurred while working as a sheriff, handling prisoners to and from the courtroom where I had met him.

Why didn't he apply for a higher rank or a higher position? Courtroom employees wondered about Joe's refusal to try to get more money and become sergeant. He was qualified, and sometimes he was actually doing the job of a superior officer.

The members at his Baptist church in Philadelphia asked similar questions after Joe, time and again, politely refused to be named a deacon. He could not give an order from any official position, he said.

His Vietnam War experience forced him to never again give orders to anyone, even those seeking spiritual advice from Joe as a deacon. That's PTSD at its worst!

One will never know what life Joe would have led had he not been stricken in war. One can only imagine after coming in contact with a guy like him.

You won't see any of Joe's injuries on first meeting him.

But they are there. They're part of his PTSD.

And some wounds never heal.

In war, truth is the first casualty.

—Aeschylus

SILVER LINING SHINES
ON DARK DAYS OF WAR

If you're like me, you need time and distance to place these events into a proper context. I carried guilt and shame for forty years, kicking myself each time a flashback appeared almost out of nowhere. Only recently have I been able to view the worst day of my life with a little more gentleness, a little more forgiveness.

I put the experience into the context of the entire war and not a few days, a few weeks, or even several months. I can now see what led up to the horrific moments and how I responded. Ironically, I now see that I had responded the same way to what has turned out to be one of the best days of my life. It was a day I pooh-poohed and made light of when it was happening.

Today I see it as a balancing of karma for me.

All those years, however, I focused on the negative, a sense of failure and loss, and refused to look at its twin brother, the positive events that reflected my success in war and filled me with good old-fashioned appreciation and respects.

It was the worst day of my life, and I blanked out details from what happened afterward. Oh, I remember the investigation and the questioning by the army, directed to look into the friendly fire accident. I told them the same story but left out the danger that I felt. Most soldiers didn't want to admit they faced fear—I'm one of them—or even how they learned to overcome that fear. Your fear was nobody's business unless it caused you to freeze and become immobile in the face of an attack. I don't know of anyone who faced this crippling shutdown. I had suspected that some of those who had been in country a long time learned to deal with it in different ways.

One skinny fellow from Kentucky with rotten black teeth would stay high while walking point. I thought he was on some type of uppers, but after speaking to a grunt in the marines, I now suspect that my point man had been eating some of the so-called psychedelic, naturally grown juju seeds or beans. You'd see many Vietnamese women—"mama-sans," we'd call them—with dark, blackened teeth. They seem to have a perpetual smile and couldn't keep their mouths shut to prevent us Westerners from seeing what appeared to be rotting teeth. They'd chew them in the field. I guess it aided in the backbreaking work most did without farm animals to assist them. You'd see them gazing almost thoughtlessly, smiling their gap-toothed and blackened smiles with nary a concern for the past or a worry about the future. They lived in another world from you and me, a world of rice paddies and the fields of Vietnam. I suspected that some of my men got high from something, but as long as it did not interfere with their job performance and our accomplishing the mission, I didn't care.

Hell, I got high in Vietnam. On the first of two trips to the capital city, Saigon, I smoked the wacky weed. I smoked it in the company of enlisted men, a real no-no for someone in the officer corps. "Fraternizing with the troops" is what they called it, even if you were with a prostitute the entire time but in the same room cordoned off by blankets hanging from the ceiling to give you a sense of privacy from the other three johns enjoying a little R & R from the field of fire. I had no idea the thing I smoked had something other than marijuana in it. I learned later it was opium, but I didn't care in that moment.

⋏　⋏　⋏

The young Vietnamese woman passed me a joint as we sat comfortably together on the bed. I had gone to Madame Dow's Tahitian Hotel, Saigon, along with a few of my men in the First Platoon and those from the Second Platoon. They knew the best places to go, and what I learned about surviving in Vietnam was that a brand-new second lieutenant should always listen to the advice of those who had seen war before you set foot into a combat zone.

So I ended up in the large bedroom with three combat-exposed brethren who knew the lay of the land and had shown me how to navigate through unknown territory. Some Asian beauty had stretched clotheslines wall to wall just several inches from the ceiling. She then placed blankets on the lines. The blankets separated and cordoned off four beds situated in the room. Years later, on seeing office cubicles squeezed side by side, I'd remember the engineering feat of the entrepreneurial Vietnamese.

The dark-haired, petite, wonderfully trained young woman soon opened herself to the fumbling and stumbling kid visiting the house, perhaps for the first time, like me. What stands out is the feeling that maybe I would never experience being with a woman again. I really believed this might be the last time because there was no guarantee you'd return from the field.

She was oh so gentle. I saw her as a gift from God. How can a God-fearing, born-again student of Buddhism, kabbalah, and the Sufi equate prostitution with the spiritual bestowal from the greatest source of love and compassion in the universe? The women knew, or had come to learn, that they too offered solace—a refuge—away from the fighting.

▲   ▲   ▲

There is a refrain from a song written about a soldier who was to have fought nearly fifty-some years ago that plays through my mind as I look back. In the verse, which was sung later by folk and country and western music performers, a French woman opens herself to a young "doughboy," a kid still in his teens who shows up at the whorehouse shy and quiet, presenting a flower to her.

He smells of some cheap wine he probably drank for the first time in his life. She is as gentle as the princess who had greeted me. He rushes to the finish line and falls into the peaceful sleep of a baby who cares not about facing the possibility of death the very next day.

She knew. She loved. She comforted. "Tonight, the War Is Over" becomes a reality in her arms and through the body she presses warm against you, mingling the uncertainty of one sentient being with the purest compassion and understanding from the other.

God, how I needed that escape! How I needed to feel this love, even though it was a one-night stand paid for through military scrip.

To be intimate with a woman, to lie with her not knowing if you'd live or die in the next few days, weeks, or months…I never wanted to leave this beautiful creature. I wanted to protect her from any harm our society would want to bring against her for peddling her wares.

She gave me a taste for life again after I had subsisted on nothing but death and destruction only a day or two earlier. She gave of herself so that an American soldier speaking a foreign tongue would taste the peace and reality of another world, a world that comes about in that moment of climax, and you become one with all there is and ever was.

I made love to her three times that night. That's three times in one night! Don't tell any of my wives, but it was some of the best sex I ever had and the most I've ever climaxed in one night. Looking at the possibility of no tomorrow can have that effect on your appreciation of today.

God bless such an immoral act!

(Madame Dow's Tahitian Hotel was closed sometime in 1975 or later when the Viet Cong occupied the city of Saigon. It may have reopened as a restaurant and museum under a different name in what is now called Ho Chi Minh City.)

Unthinking respect for authority is the greatest enemy of truth.

—Albert Einstein

SAIGON REVISITED

Some forty years after my visit to Madam Dow's Tahitian Hotel in Saigon (now Ho Chi Minh City), I found myself talking about the Vietnamese city with a spiritual instructor who I later learned had served in the Vietnam War. I had watched Wilhelm through an internet hookup—he taught kabbalah—and felt an immediate kinship to him. Turns out he was a medic, having served in the military, and was a Vietnam veteran, like me. He often spoke of higher worlds those of us could attain if we but opened ourselves to the wisdom of the teachings and a teacher. You needed to open when a "point in the heart" urges or pulls you to seek answers to life's most puzzling questions: "Who am I?" "Why am I here?" "What is the purpose of life?"

(Through my exposure to Buddhism, Sufism, and the kabbalah, I've learned they pretty much point in the same direction, and that is something I learned from the old Baltimore Catechism in first or second grade: my purpose is to know, love, and serve God no matter how I perceive that unperceivable Higher Being to be...or in the Buddhist perspective, not to be.)

While at a spiritual conference, I overheard my internet mentor telling a story to a fellow at an adjoining table.

"I made Spec-5 three times," he said.

"Wait a minute," my eavesdropping mind said to myself. "How the hell can you be promoted to Specialist 5 three times?"

Never having been formally introduced to Wilhelm, I nevertheless broke into the conversation and demanded to know how such a military achievement could be accomplished.

"I was demoted. Twice," he explained to me, a total stranger.

He solidified the camaraderie I felt for him with his story about "being busted" when arriving back to camp later than the time his pass entitled him to return. He was not demoted because he was late, he said. He was demoted because he got into an accident on returning to camp.

The next demotion occurred when Wilhelm, the army medic, disagreed with the medical procedure that some nonmedical army captain insisted Wilhelm apply in a combat situation.

"I'm not going to do it," Wilhelm told his superior officer. He'd told his commanding officer how much harm following that order would generate, and Wilhelm hoped the captain would concur with his expertise. The captain did not and insisted Wilhelm follow orders. Wilhelm stuck to his principles.

"Fuck you. I'm not going to do it," Wilhelm said with all the military bearing he could muster.

"You say that one more time, I'm going to bust you," the captain replied.

"Fuck you," Wilhelm said with all the charm of an Irishman who had just kissed the Blarney Stone and removed any malice from his heart.

The captain busted him. Later, the higher command learned what the captain was trying to do—it may have had something to do with increasing the so-called body count—and the commanding officer's orders were rescinded.

But what made me see Wilhelm as a blood brother was when I discovered we shared the same memories of that place in Saigon that had provided the needed succor to the young men facing combat day in and day out.

"Ever make it to Saigon?" I asked the spiritual leader.

"Yes," he said with a certain look in his eye.

"Oh, those Saigon nights," I said. I don't know what got into me, but I went into my story about the house of ill repute I had visited. I didn't say it in a bragging way but in a wistful, warm, and friendly way.

"Was the place called Madame Dow's Tahitian Hotel?" Wilhelm asked.

"I don't know," I answered.

"Were the rooms with the ladies of the night above a restaurant?" he quizzed me further.

"Yeah," I said, excitement growing. "It was on the second floor."

I was elated. Here I was, seeking a higher path to my life only to find out the man I'd chosen to help guide me had walked the same road I had walked some forty years earlier. There was no guilt, no shame, and no remorse, and

I felt an understanding come over me that had to have manifested from the Source of all understanding.

It turned out that Wilhelm had been in the same building I had visited but only a year earlier. What a coincidence. What synchronicity! As a medic, Wilhelm helped protect the "privates" of many a soldier, sailor, airman, and marine that might have made their way into the arms of the working women there. He ensured they passed medical tests to prevent the spread of disease. Good commanders in every war know not only how to accomplish their mission but also how to provide for the physical and emotional welfare of their men.

Where do you think we got the term "hookers" as a euphemism for prostitutes? It came from the American Civil War. The camp followers of the Union Army got that nickname when they aided soldiers under General Hooker. The name "hookers" referred to those who openly took the men's minds away from the slog of war week after week, month after month, year after year. My God! How many years did a tour of duty consist of in the Civil War? What about the Korean War and World War I and World War II? The soldiers were in it for the duration. Even though the Vietnam War would drag on to become the longest war in American history (at the time), a tour of duty lasted only a year.

How would a soldier like to have served in the European Ten Years' War? How about the war between the Greeks and the Trojans, the story told in the *Iliad*, that lasted ten years? Worse yet, what type of hell do you think warriors among the French and English faced during a skirmish called the Hundred Years' War?

Peace! How many wars were waged in thy name?

—Alexander Pope

TO DREAM THE IMPOSSIBLE DREAM

It's ironic that I can use the wisdom from Buddhism's tenet of nonviolence to apply it to perhaps the most violent time of my life. There is nothing whatsoever nonviolent about being a soldier. Your purpose for living is to protect others and kill if necessary. I was trained to inflict harm on anyone threatening my men or my platoon. I was a product of the US Army. I wanted to be a good soldier, and unfortunately, that meant learning how to inflict pain on others. Not by my own intent but through the orders of others—my superior officers, my country, my American way of life.

How is it that a person can give his life for another with love and compassion in a nonviolent way and be called a saint but be labeled a sinner while giving his life in combat while brutally taking the lives of his enemy?

Isn't the intent the same?

You act out of love for another, whether it's back home at a peace march or in the jungle fighting for a cause most of your fellow countrymen deemed worthy enough to send you to war over.

Don't know of anyone who ever aspired to be a bad soldier. We wanted to do right by our country and to take seriously our oath to the American Constitution. As an officer, I took just as seriously my oath to try to accomplish the mission and look out for the welfare of the men. Even under impossible conditions, I always tried to do good, to do the right thing.

I still remember our graduation from Fort Benning, Georgia, when we were to be commissioned following six months of Officer Candidate School.

One of the more musically talented cadets sang the popular song from the *Don Quixote* musical called *Man of La Mancha*. It was our ambition—no, our divine aspiration:

To fight for the right without question or pause
To march into hell for a heavenly cause…

It was this desire and idealism that got me into wanting to be a leader in the first place. It is what has sustained me the many times I felt I had failed not only others but also myself.

▲   ▲   ▲

The military investigation into the mortar round falling on my troops concluded that I, the lieutenant, was at fault for the friendly fire. I don't remember the details. They're unimportant now. A kind supervisor told me that a major deciding factor was the future aspects of the two parties involved: me and the sergeant who was then in charge of the mortar platoon. The sergeant was what we called a career soldier, one who planned to serve his entire life in the military. He was some eight to ten years in by then and was on his way to at least a twenty-year career.

The lieutenant was a soldier who had been drafted and wanted nothing more to do with the restrictive life of the army. This helped to appease me. Looking back, I see it doesn't really matter anymore. On leaving the army, I entered college and got a journalism degree, then a master's degree in American history, before working as a newspaper reporter, a union organizer, and, for the last twenty years of my work life, a public defender.

I don't think I'd have ever become a Philadelphia lawyer had I not been able to dream that so-called impossible dream or try "to bear with unbearable sorrow" the hand that life had dealt me when I was twenty-one years old.

War…is harmful not only to the conquered but to the conqueror.

—Ludwig von Mises

BREATHE REALLY EASY.
NOW...SHOOT!

I could never figure out how a city boy who had never shot a gun in his life could get the army's highest medal for marksmanship with a rifle. But there I was in Fort Bragg, North Carolina, mowing down one bull's-eye after another as if I were the reincarnation of Sergeant York of World War I fame.

Years later I realized it was all in the breathing. When you take aim, you have to relax and slowly squeeze the trigger. Any sudden movement or jarring of the slightest bit will cause the aim to go off, and you'd shoot off target. I was and still am an excellent breather. I can meditate with the best of them, at least for a short period of time—say, up to a half an hour, maybe sixty minutes at tops.

The secret is to simply let go. Let go of all thoughts and focus on the target to a point where you become one with it. You melt into the rifle, and it becomes an appendage of you, a third arm and another hand to deliver an object to a certain location somewhere in the distance. With my left eye closed, my right one would take in the sights of the weapon and match the target and my view of the target precisely with what I wanted to hit down-field of the rifle range. Firing came almost on reflex to me, as if I were simply remembering how to ride a bicycle from some previous kid's life.

I'd squeeze the trigger ever so gently, as if I were touching a baby. The rifle would recoil, and my shoulder would take the impact as I'd ready myself to go for the next round and the next until my day at the range was completed. Damned if I didn't score one of the highest marks in my basic training platoon! I was awarded the sharpshooter medal, above such medals given for excellence as a marksman and even an expert.

I never liked the M16 rifle. Most soldiers who were good marksmen didn't either. It always felt like a toy gun made by Mattel. The M14 had weight to it, and many a man who became a sniper would swear by them.

The lighter M16 was good for close-range fire, either single shot or semi-automatic. I would never, however, like to have my life depend on one for its accuracy beyond fifty meters.

Other weapons I learned to fire included the M60 machine gun and the grenade launcher as well as the M80, the small bazooka-like, one-shot piece that I never saw used in Vietnam. How could you fire one in the jungle? The round would hit low-hanging branches and explode right in front of you. I never engaged in a battle on an open field. I fought only in triple-canopy jungle where small arms bullets could easily pass through bushes, hanging branches, and vegetation.

I can't remember much of my training with artillery and mortar weapons. I did learn to read coordinates and plot them on a map. I got fairly good with directions and recognizing the topography. (It's ironic how much mortars would figure in my tour of duty in Vietnam, creating in part the worst day of my life and then later one of the best days.)

That was pretty much the extent of my weapons training when circumstances came together, creating the very worst day I would ever encounter.

(That day and the men I served with who would never come back haunt me. Their memories arise around holidays recognizing servicemen and on those occasions when I open myself to somewhere deep inside that still needs some sort of healing. The following is something I experienced when walking a labyrinth, an experience I recommend servicepeople, as well as noncombatants of all stripes, engage in to help clear their hearts and minds.)

Do not waste time bothering whether you "love" your neighbor; act as if you did.

—C.S. Lewis

INTERLUDE (FAST FORWARD NO. 2):

LABYRINTH OPENS A HIDDEN MAZE INSIDE ME

https://contoveros.com/2010/07/12/
labyrinth-opens-a-hidden-maze-inside-me/

I walked a labyrinth and stepped into Vietnam last night. Trouble is that forty years after the war, I liked it. I did not want to leave the maze despite what lay ahead. Strangely, I felt safe there. Secure in my skills. I didn't want to come home. Just like years earlier.

The good news is I should be able to put the war behind me. The bad news is that I'll have the memories wherever I go.

I didn't expect a flashback to occur when I entered the grasslands surrounding the labyrinth in Lansdale, Pennsylvania, twenty-five miles outside of Philadelphia. I'd walked several before, finding release and calm in the walk itself and a feeling of accomplishment in reaching an end point at the center of the maze. In this case, it was a huge gray boulder in the middle of a field of high grass mixed with small flowers growing wild in Stony Creek Park.

Six of us met prior to the walk as our spiritual leader, Tracie Nichols, gathered us in a circle. She faced the setting sun and asked us to listen to the earth call to us. I felt a tug from my soul and chose to go first. I had walked point sometimes while leading a combat platoon several decades earlier. I could do it again.

I began the trek, slowly moving one foot after another, dragging my big toe as my leg swept the earth beneath before placing my foot squarely in front of me. It's part of a walking meditation I learned from my Zen teacher two years earlier and from a Buddhist monk I made offerings with at Omega Institute in upstate New York.

He had served in Vietnam as a helicopter gunner and dedicated his life to helping veterans with posttraumatic stress (PTSD but without the "disorder" part).

My thoughts slowed, and I walked peacefully on the path bordered by grass patches two to three feet high in some areas. I saw worn spots in the path, lines of trodden dirt where others had walked before. Birds called from nearby trees, and you could hear the cascading of water from a fountain that spewed water into the air and onto a pond less than twenty feet away.

Insects greeted me some fifteen to twenty feet into the walk. I took little notice of 'em, remembering them from the boonies in Vietnam. Plus I'm practicing Buddhism now, and we revere all life, including that of the mosquito world.

I hadn't walked more than ten steps when a member of our group passed me. The path was wide enough for two to walk abreast, with a little squeezing here and there. I did not mind. Tracie instructed us to walk our own pace and to walk by another if we so felt drawn.

Soon I realized all others had walked by me. It was then that I returned to Vietnam. I remembered walking paths just like this one. High grass on one side and a wooded area all around you.

My focus was on the ground while meditating this way. It's called "walking meditation." Hands held together and across my chest had morphed into an M16 semiautomatic rifle like the one I carried as a first lieutenant. A twenty-one-year-old who discovered peace in that world despite the firefights he—I should say, I—knew would occur.

You learned to appreciate the moment more. Feel life like you had never felt it before and rarely would afterward. It was a flashback that turned into a glorious moment of peace.

It was serene. Comfortable. Secure to know skills I developed and learned would serve me well. To always be on guard. Be hyperalert. Hypervigilant.

Trust my instincts to take quick action and not freeze or, worse yet, flee. Airborne! All the way, sir! Fleeing's not in my makeup. Face the challenge head-on and deal with it, accomplishing the mission while also looking out for the welfare of your men.

You don't know how simple it made life there in the bush. Things were black or white with few, if any, shades of gray. We were the good guys. The others, the bad. You believed, if needed, you'd give your own life to save that of your buddy. Nothing to do with patriotism or "my country, right or wrong." I guess you could say it was out of love and compassion for a guy who might end up saving your life. He always protected your back as you did his.

Too soon, those beliefs would be tested on returning home. There's no buddy system in civilian life. No need to quickly fire on an enemy at the least provocation. No market for ex-GIs trained to use killing force to bring battles to an end.

But all of that stuff remains inside of you, doesn't it, LT? That's the name my troops called me: "LT," short for "lieutenant." Learned some leadership traits, thanks to Vietnam. I discovered that I couldn't shake 'em back here in the States, and looking back, I see where I tried to continue using them in some career choices: union organizer and activist, college newspaper editor, and finally attorney leading a defendant through a maze we call the practice of law.

It all came back to me while walking the labyrinth. All of my men came back. None got killed under my command, thank God.

I've always been proud of that fact, but what reared its ugly head was a reminder that not everyone was as lucky. Like two guys in Second Platoon who were killed when setting up an ambush only to walk into a trip wire that exploded a Claymore mine.

I fell to the ground when I saw some small wildflowers in the maze. I picked some as tears poured out mixed with the messy stuff that I felt coming out of my nose.

Sobbing, I remembered Lt. Victor Lee Ellinger, Third Platoon leader from Staunton, Virginia. His killing by the Viet Cong haunts me today.

Getting up, I wiped my nose. To hell with my eyes.

"Finish this goddamn walk," I said, determined to push on like I did when the hurt first came and I could not show the emotion or the pain because I was in charge and had to show a good example, to bear up under such circumstances.

I walked the maze with more vigor, more purpose, with my head held a little higher. Seeing the finish line and the main goal, the center of the maze, I fell to the ground again, throwing my arms around the boulder and crying, this time with a smile stretched across my face.

You made it, Michael J. You're going to live and tell your story. You'll eat pepperoni pizza and see beautiful women of all shapes and sizes in flowing summer dresses whom you'll fall in love with because of a love you share.

Tracie Nichols told us that we could leave behind what we had experienced in the labyrinth. She said it had something to do with the solar eclipse and the new moon. Yet the seeds we planted, the hopes we raised, would continue to flourish when the full moon appeared two weeks later, she added.

I'll be back. Sans these Vietnam souvenirs. And with a new resolve to continue on this journey with a lighter heart and more compassion for what seekers find within their maze.

All wars are civil wars, because all men are brothers.

—François Fénelon

PINNED FOR A LIFE ABOVE AND BEYOND THE CALL

https://contoveros.com/2012/04/28/
pinned-for-a-life-above-beyond-the-call/

While Neil Armstrong had just taken a giant leap for all mankind, I took a small step toward adulthood one month after the moon landing, and I had no one to thank for it except my brother, who encouraged me to aim for the stars in becoming an officer and a gentleman in the army of the United States of America.

I had weathered the worst six months of my life, worse even than my later combat duty in Vietnam, as I underwent the rigorous training in Officer Candidate School. We ran everywhere we went, and when we couldn't run anymore, we'd run in place, waiting in line for chow outside the mess hall or to use the latrine. I was the second youngest in a company of some two hundred recruits—carrying a minimum rank of Specialist Five (E-5)—who learned tactics and survival skills and how to endure under the harshest conditions while developing leadership qualities. The youngest ones were targeted for even more physical and psychological drills because of our age.

The company commander once ordered me to do four hundred sit-ups in a sleeping bag, relenting only after he got tired of counting, and I tore parts of my butt apart from sliding it back and forth against the ground so much. I'm surprised I didn't tear a hole through the bag, but instead of forcing me out of the program, it encouraged me not to quit and to take whatever he was willing to dish out. At age twenty, with nothing but a high school diploma, I earned the respect of several with college and graduate degrees who might have changed their minds about my leading troops.

Those of us who made it filed out of the auditorium at Fort Benning, Georgia, having been addressed by some old, weathered colonel who appeared to be in his seventies and was still jumping out of airplanes, his latest count reaching more than six hundred jumps! He looked a little crazy, "gung ho crazy," if you know what I mean. His eyes seemed permanently fixed wide open; he was jumpy and alert to the smallest sound or movement nearby. I would compare his demeanor and makeup to the hyperawareness and sensitivity I'd get from posttraumatic stress years later.

But on this day, August 22, 1969, my oldest brother had prepared a ceremony to take place outside the doors of the graduation hall. Dressed in his regular working uniform as an E-6 (staff sergeant), he carefully removed two metal bars from a cardboard box. We called them "butter bars." The yellow metal bars symbolized the rank of second lieutenant, the lowest rank in the army's officer corps.

So many things went through my mind as I stood at attention, looking straight ahead, hoping my dress uniform hat was affixed properly. I didn't want to be out of order in any way, shape, or form at this time in my life. What a moment!

My oldest brother, six years my senior, was about to pin the bars onto my shoulder, officially welcoming me to a world where I would become an officer and a gentleman. I did not know then what the designation by an act of Congress would actually mean. That would come later in Vietnam, when I'd see mortar fire hit and wound half a squad I was leading; when a Viet Cong sniper would shoot and kill Lt. Vic Ellinger, one of only three lieutenants in our combat infantry company; or as two soldiers under another lieutenant's command would forget where they had placed their Claymore mine trip wire and walk into it, killing themselves.

That was all in the future, along with the PTSD that would raise its ugly head some twenty-five years after the war. It wouldn't be all bad, particularly right after being discharged, when this young veteran would use a sense of failure to achieve success in academics, getting degrees in journalism and history before finding his other life's calling years later as a public defender trial lawyer after obtaining a Juris Doctor degree.

I knew none of this as my brother George fastened the metal bars to my uniform jacket, stepped back, and brought his right hand briskly to his forehead, saluting the superior officer that I had become.

It was a shining moment of my life. One of only a few I would ever experience.

We used to wonder where war lived, what it was that made it so vile. And now we realize that we know where it lives...inside ourselves.

—Albert Camus

GLOSSARY OF A
WAR SPELLED OUT
IN MEMORIES

There are certain words and phrases that anyone whose set foot in Vietnam during the war years will never forget. I'm willing to bet that they get what psychologists call a flashback. That is, our minds go back to the time or times that we heard the words for the first time or to that particular setting when they imprinted somewhere in our psyches.

"No sweat, GI." I don't know when I first heard it, perhaps while in basic. That's another term we used. Instead of saying "basic training," we shortened it to "basic." No matter which way you cut it, however, it was an eight-week trial by fire by some of the meanest sons of bitches ever to don a drill sergeant's hat. They were trying their best to force boys into becoming men fighting men who would obey orders and act as a unit with their fellow GIs.

"GI" is the term used for "government issue," and I believe the phrase was shortened and used first to designate the soldiers fighting in World War II. Earlier, those fearless young men fighting in the trenches of Europe in World War I were known as doughboys.

OK, now you want to know more about doughboys. Well, according to military sources left unnamed, "doughboy" was an informal term for a member of the US Army and the Marine Corps. But the term dates back to the Mexican War of 1846–48. It was still used as late as World War II. (Doughboys, incidentally, were usually the youngest men, who had dropped out of school and joined the army. The term was gradually replaced during World War II by "GI.") Observers of the soldiers in the Mexican War noticed the infantrymen were constantly covered with chalky dust from marching through the dry terrain of Mexico. They looked like men made up of unbaked dough. (Does the "Pillsbury Doughboy" give you some idea of what a slim one might have looked like?)

Other sources said the dust-covered infantry soldiers resembled the mud bricks of the area, known as "adobes." Still others claimed the term came from the method of cooking field rations using flour and rice baked in the ashes of their campfire.

"Grunt" was the name used to describe infantry platoon soldiers, who proudly cherished the title. Although I was an officer, I first saw myself as a grunt, particularly when "humping" the boonies, at times walking "point." (See definitions later in this chapter.) The word was another slang term the military used to describe the infantrymen, the foot soldiers of the war. They were "straight leg," meaning they were not "airborne," that is, jumping out of airplanes as parachutists did in previous wartime engagements. A grunt walked everywhere he went, except when he was "choppered in" by a helicopter to an LZ (landing zone).

I believe it was a derogatory comment at first. Soldiers were known to grunt like pigs when they had to get up from the ground where they had been resting, place a rucksack on their bag weighing some thirty pounds, and hump the boonies. ("Hump" simply means to walk slowly with total concentration while on patrol, often in triple-canopy jungle, which we commonly called the "boonies" or "boondocks." See below.)

▲ ▲ ▲

Here is how the Urban Dictionary defines the word "grunt":

> The term "grunt" is used in the military as a general term for someone who has an MOS (Military Occupational Specialty) for the "Infantry." In the Marine Corps, all MOS's preceded by the number "03" are Infantry. About as "grunt" as you can get in the Corps is "031— Basic Rifleman."

The opposite of a "grunt" is a "Poague," a derogatory reference to pretty much anyone who isn't a grunt that is normally reserved for Marines who work in an office or some other rear-echelon job as part of their regular duties ("In the rear with the gear"). Call a Poague a "grunt," and they love it, but call a grunt a "Poague" and see what happens.

In my outfit of grunts, we called those serving in the base camps and in the relatively more secure rear areas "REMFs." It stood for "Rear Echelon Motherfuckers."

⟁ ⟁ ⟁

I was flabbergasted when an editor who had read one of my stories on the Vietnam War asked me what I meant by a boonie hat. I tried to describe it as best I could but was unable to come up with the origin of the headgear. (I hope my next editor approves because I'm explaining it to her now!)

A boonie hat is a form of wide-brim hat commonly used by soldiers and marines in the military forces. A fabric band of branch loops is normally sewn around the crown of the hat. That section is meant to hold vegetation to use as a camouflage. In addition, a strap provided security but was hardly ever used, in my experience. I believe the US Army Green Berets first began to use them during the Vietnam War. The initial hats were made from salvaged materials from other uniform items or even from a former parachute.

The name itself is comes from the word "boonie," which is the abbreviated form of "boondocks." That word in itself is military slang from the word "bundok," which I believe might mean "mountain" in some Asian language.

In 1967, the "Summer of Love," the US Army began issuing boonie hats as the "Hat, Jungle, with Insect Net." They were made of cotton and wind-resistant poplin in beautifully drab olive coloring. The boonie hat was often worn with the wearer's rank insignia imprinted on the front above the branch loops.

WORDS OF WISDOM FROM THE WAR

There was one word and a special date that every soldier who served in the Vietnam War held sacred. That was his DEROS date. "DEROS" stood for "date of expected return from overseas." Many in the rear would have the date circled in red ink on calendars with elaborate plans to undertake as soon as the date got near. All American soldiers believed that they would eventually face their DEROS.

Some did not. Others became afraid of the date as it drew near, realizing they would be leaving behind a piece of themselves that they had lost while war transformed them from a child to a man.

ᛉ   ᛉ   ᛉ

C-4 plastic is the name of the putty substance that was packed into Claymore mines. It was an explosive material that was white and gummy-like. It would explode when triggered by some sort of electrical device that was usually hooked up to a trip wire.

All of the infantry soldiers were required to carry it at one time or another. The C-4 burned like a sterno can when it was lit. It was the best thing I ever used to heat coffee while in the field. You simply cut open the back of the hard plastic covering of the Claymore mine and extracted the material with the same knife, usually a hunting knife. (I never cut the mines, but one of the Kit Carson scouts assigned to my platoon did and would use it to heat instant coffee for me in the mornings.) Others used the C-4 to heat meats and tuna fish delivered in their C rations.

ᛉ   ᛉ   ᛉ

Oh yeah, C rations were "combat rations." (I think some of the ones we got were left over from World War II!) The rations consisted of a can of mixed meat or tuna and cans of fruit, some type of dessert, a pack of powdered cocoa, a pack of four cigarettes, and two pieces of chewing gum.

ᛉ   ᛉ   ᛉ

The following are some of the words and phrases Vietnam War veterans can easily recall. They are provided to you by *The Sixties Project*, sponsored by Viet Nam Generation and the Institute of Advanced Technology in the Humanities at the University of Virginia at Charlottesville.

Diddy-bopping: Walking carelessly.

Didi: Slang from the Vietnamese word "di," meaning "to leave" or "to go."

Didi mau: Vietnamese slang for "go quickly," as in "you better didi mau, mother-humper!"

Dinky dau: To be crazy. Usually followed by someone making a circular motion with his index finger at his temple.

Dust-off: Medical evacuation by helicopter.

Eleven Bravo: The MOS of an infantryman.

ETS: The date of departure for overseas duty station; estimated time of separation from military service.

Fatigues: Standard combat uniform, green in color.

Firefight: A battle or exchange of small arms fire with the enemy.

Frag: Fragmentation grenade; verb form of "fragging."

Fragging: Assassination of an officer by his own troops, usually by a grenade.

Freak: Radio frequency. Also, a "junkie" or a "doper."

Freq: Radio frequency.

Friendly fire: Accidental attacks on US or allied soldiers by other US or allied soldiers.

FUBAR: Acronym for "fucked up beyond all recognition," used to describe any disorganized operation.

Ho Chi Minh slippers: Sandals made from tires. The soles are made from the tread and the straps from inner tubes. (I owned a pair of 'em.)

Hooch: A hut or simple dwelling, either military or civilian. Also spelled "hootch."

Horn: Radio microphone.

Hot: Area under fire.

Hump: March or hike carrying a rucksack; to perform any arduous task.

Jody: The person who wins your lover or spouse away while you are in the Nam. From the marching song or cadence count "Ain't no use in goin' home / Jody's got your girl and gone / Sound off..."

Jungle boots: Footwear that looks like a combination of a combat boot and canvas sneaker used by the US military in a tropical climate where leather rots because of the dampness. The canvas structure also speeds drying after crossing streams, rice paddies, and so on.

Klick: Kilometer.

KIA: Killed in action.

LZ: Landing zone, usually a small clearing secured temporarily for the landing of resupply helicopters. Some become more permanent and eventually become base camps.

Mama-san: Pidgin used by American servicemen for any older Vietnamese woman. ("Baby-san" referred to a young girl, while "papa-san" referred to an older man.)

Million-dollar wound: A noncrippling wound serious enough to warrant return to the United States.

MOS: Military occupational specialty.

Number one: The best.

Number ten: The worst.

P-38: A tiny collapsible can opener, also known as a "John Wayne."

R & R: A break from the war for relaxation and recuperation.

Shake 'n' bake: Sergeant who attended NCO school and earned rank after only a very short time in uniform. (They were among the best I ever met!)

Short: A term used by everyone in Vietnam to tell all who would listen that his tour was almost over.

Short-timer: Soldier nearing the end of his tour in Vietnam.

Tee-tee: Pidgin for "very small."

⋏　⋏　⋏

Now, please turn to the next chapter and let me describe the Vietnam War by the numbers. It all started for most of us with a "1-A" or a "4-F." I was 1-A but would have paid off anyone to have gotten a coveted 4-F rating, which meant you were unfit for service in the eyes of our favorite war hawks of the day.

(Did you know that former vice president Dick Cheney never served one day in combat, gaining five — count 'em, *five* — deferments, thus keeping him out of the front lines where he would eventually place millions of young men without deferments in harm's way in a place called Iraq?)

Today the real test of power is not capacity to make war but capacity to prevent it.

—Anne O'Hare McCormick

GREETINGS! THIS IS UNCLE SAM ON DRAFT DAY

The Selective Service System is an agency of the United States government that maintains information on those subject to military conscription. Most male and male immigrant noncitizens between the ages of eighteen and twenty-five are required by law to have registered within thirty days of their eighteenth birthdays. In addition, you have to notify the Selective Service of any changes to the information you provided for your registration cards, like a change of address. The government estimated in 2010 that it had the names of more than sixteen million men on file.

▲　▲　▲

According to Department of Defense records, the Selective Service System was created in 1917, enabling the government to conscript men for military service. At that time all males aged twenty-one to thirty were required to register for a service period of twelve months. As of mid-November 1917, all registrants were placed in one of five new classifications.

Men in Class 1 were the first to be drafted. The lucky men in lower classifications were deferred. In addition, there were "dependency deferments" for registrants who were fathers and/or husbands. For some reason, the age limit was later raised in August 1918 to a maximum age of forty-five. That draft was discontinued in 1920.

The Selective Service System was resurrected in 1940, and by 1948, the government created a new and separate system, which became the basis for the modern system.

▲　▲　▲

In 1968, the year that I was drafted, all men were given a rating by the system. Among the classifications were the following:

1-A: Those eligible for military service (like yours truly).

1-AO: Conscientious objector who is available for noncombatant military service.

1-O: Conscientious objector to all military service. (If you plead this, you have to prove your objection is based upon moral, ethical, or religious beliefs that play a significant role in your life. In addition, one has to show that his objection is not confined to a particular war. The person still has to serve in alternative service.)

1-S (H): Student deferred by statute (he's still in high school). Induction into the military could be deferred until graduation or until reaching the age of twenty.

1-S (C): Student deferred by statute (he's still in college). Induction could be deferred to the end of the current semester if an undergraduate or until the end of the academic year if he's a senior.

1-W: Conscientious objector ordered to perform alternative service.

1-Y: Those available for military service but qualified only in case of war or a national emergency. (This was usually given to young men with medical conditions that were "limiting but not disabling." It was discontinued in 1971 and its members were reclassified as 4-F.)

2-A: These were deferred because of civilian occupation (nonagricultural).

2-B: These were deferred because of occupation in a war industry, such as defense contract work.

2-C: These got deferred because of agricultural occupation.

2-D: This was for divinity students. The deferment lasted until graduation or until the student reached twenty-four years old.

2-S: They got deferred because of collegiate study. Their deferment lasted either until graduation or until the student reached twenty-four years of age.

3-A: They got deferred because of hardship to dependents.

4-D: Minister of religion who has formally been ordained by a recognized religion and is serving as a full-time minister with a church and congregation.

4-E: Conscientious objectors who opposed both combatant and noncombatant training and service. Alternative service was still required.

4-F: Not acceptable for military service. To be eligible, a person must have been found not qualified for service under the established physical, mental, or moral standards.

4-G: A person was exempted from service because of the death of a parent or a sibling while serving, or whose parent or sibling has been a prisoner of war (POW) or missing in action (MIA).

America will never be destroyed from the outside. If we falter and lose our freedoms, it will be because we destroyed ourselves.

—Abraham Lincoln

SHERMAN'S PURPLE HEART AND MY BSA

If you served in the infantry, you would have heard the term "50-cal," which referred to the .50 caliber machine gun that all platoons carried. I usually fostered it on the biggest grunt I could find, letting him choose assistants to help him carry the rounds for the gun.

Sherman was one of my machine gunners. He was only five feet, nine inches tall but was broad in the chest and looked like he could carry a load. He was from the Midwest, with a midwestern accent. He'd get all red in the face from marching long distances and was always the first to hit the ground whenever we'd take a break; he was among the last to get up, grunting the way that some people claim the grunts got their names: by grunting or complaining about being forced to do something he didn't want to do!

I'll never forget pulling guard duty at a base camp over a three-day visit. I found two prostitutes in a bunker with two soldiers and, rather than discipline them, I got a soldier with a jeep to escort the young girls to other bunkers to help the men relieve their war tensions. When it came for me to take part, I politely declined, ending up being called "Cheap-cheap Charlie" by one of the Vietnamese women. (That means "frugal" in my book but "Number 10" in a young woman's book. Number 10 means "Cheap-cheap Charlie," according to a hooker in Vietnam.)

On the last night, our camp was attacked with mortars by an unseen enemy. Sherman was sharing one of the bunkers with another member of the platoon when we got "incoming." That's the term we used for incoming fire from the enemy, and in this case, it referred to missiles that the Viet Cong had fired at us.

Sherman was wearing his boonie hat when he jumped to his feet, striking the top of his head, which caused bleeding. He got treated for the injury the next day, I recall, long after the brief shelling had ended and things had returned to normal.

Well, Sherman put in for and got a Purple Heart out of the deal. Technically, he deserved it. We were under fire and he was responding to the enemy when he got wounded while securing his position during the attack. I can't fault him for putting in for it. I wouldn't have, but that's just me, if you know what I mean.

▲   ▲   ▲

Staying with the numbers, there was something I had never seen while in active service, but always "heard tell" about. It was your 201 file, a US Army personnel file. I likened it to what the Catholic nuns used to tell us about our permanent records. It included all of your training, your awards, and your assignments. I guess if you were disciplined for infractions, they would show up, as did your eventual discharge from the military and whether it was honorable or dishonorable.

For the longest time, I couldn't understand the acronym on one of the medals I was awarded. It wasn't until I was into my third career stateside, serving as a public defender in the Philadelphia court system, that I learned when the government issued me the actual award.

I got a BSA. You read that right! To me, it sounded like the "Boy Scouts of America" or the "Best Shooting Association" or something like that. I was a great shot, after all, and I write about that here. (See next chapter.)

I had gotten some ribbons after the war, but I wanted nothing to do with the army when I returned to civilian life. It wasn't until a neighbor who had served in a noncombat position in the Korean War told me I could get the medals for free by contacting the Veterans Administration.

I did one day. I thought it might be something nice to pass onto my son Nicholas, who was in his early teens at the time.

ʎ   ʎ   ʎ

The following is a story I wrote about the experience, followed by comments.

The world is a dangerous place, not because of those who do evil, but because of those who look on and do nothing.

—Albert Einstein

KEEPING ALL ALIVE: A LIFETIME ACHIEVEMENT

https://contoveros.com/2012/04/12/
keeping-all-alive-a-lifetime-achievement/)

After serving in the Vietnam War, I turned my back on anything having to do with the military, so I was totally surprised years later when requesting my medals. I got one that I still don't believe I earned.

How antiwar was I? Well, I joined the Vietnam Veterans against the War, providing funds for a yearly membership. I wrote against the war in my college newspaper, where I scribed as a reporter and then editor who eventually endorsed George McGovern for president of the United States against Richard Nixon and whatever secret plan Nixon said he had to end the war. (My mom had voted for Nixon four years earlier to keep me out of the draft and out of harm's way. The president didn't end the war, however; he escalated it!)

I stayed away from the Veterans of Foreign Wars and the American Legion because the members reminded me of old men who fought in "good" wars, particularly those veterans of World War II. They drank and reminisced about the glory of war, a concept that ended with the first casualty I witnessed on the battlefield. I saw no glory in fighting and only "got up for battle" when attacked and forced to come to the aid of a fellow soldier as adrenaline kicked in, and I'd do anything to protect my men.

Looking back (and this gets a little painful; I don't recommend too many combat veterans do this outside of a support group), I realized that I fought in nine or ten major engagements. We called them firefights. No one in my platoon was ever killed. We never captured any enemy alive, although we obtained their munitions, food, and supplies. I loathed the battalion commander who pushed for a higher body count, and he remains one of only two persons I find difficult to forgive for his life's actions.

So when I opened the box with the medals sent to me by the army, it was surprising to see two that I was not aware of. I was proud of the Combat Infantryman Badge, the CIB, which denotes that the wearer faced combat. I also liked the wings I earned for undergoing paratrooper training and jumping out of airplanes without breaking any legs.

But one of the new medals was given for flight into enemy territory. I earned a medal for the many times I climbed on the helicopter and took off, flying into a landing zone not knowing who or what would greet me. You've seen those pictures from the war. Every time they're shown on television, I remember being the young man who felt no fear jumping off a chopper and making his way to a secure area before determining whether it was clear for others to move on. (You couldn't pay me enough money to do it again.)

The real surprise was the other medal. For years I never knew what certain abbreviations on my discharge papers (DD-214) had stood for. I thought the medal was one of several that everyone got for stepping foot into Vietnam, something like an individual service medal unique to the zone of operation, like the European theater or the Pacific theater of World War II.

The letters were BSA. The medal could have been for getting one of the highest grades on the rifle range while in basic training. I shot with precision, earning a sharpshooter or expert badge, which were two or three rankings higher than a marksman.

I got the highest score in physical training during one extensive training session, missing a perfect rating by only eight out of five hundred points because I ran a mile in six minutes and eighteen seconds and not a flat six minutes.

Could "BSA" be the "Best Student Award?"

No, it was the Bronze Star Award.

I don't know why I got it. But it has my name engraved on the back of a metal star apparently made of bronze hung below a colorful red and blue ribbon. I don't think I deserved it. My greatest accomplishment was to keep me and everyone who ever served with me alive.

Come to think of it, I'd gladly accept that kind of award anytime—to stay alive and flourish in peacetime or in war.

FIVE COMMENTS ON "KEEPING ALL ALIVE: A LIFETIME ACHIEVEMENT"

04/16/2012 at 07:19
Souldipper says:

Michael J., you amaze me. I am writing with tears in my eyes. You are wise to be a light at the tip of the candle. Every vet I've known says nothing, and none of it was real for me. I was touched by a Canadian vet as a little girl. A poor soul lived in an old shack in Nowhere, Alberta where he could be most protected from loud noises. As a kid, I watched him when he came into town where he spoke little to anyone. Mom had explained enough to me that my heart went out to him.

Is that what he fought for? To live like a hermit out of embarrassment that he may flip out in front of peace-loving people? How the hell did we help? Probably in no way. I can only hope some of the adults said, "Thank you."

And you, Michael J. I cannot imagine your journey from that determined young editor, writing against war, to the guy who jumped out of choppers to determine an "all clear." Then to see your comrades wounded.

It's one thing to have to act in a situation that is contrary to one's belief. But the extent to which war and all its atrocities takes a human is beyond my comprehension.

I met a number of people who left the US to live in Canada to avoid the draft. I never believed they live without conscience, no matter how strongly they spoke about their actions.

One VN Vet lived up the road from me here on my island. He was a member of our Coast Guard. Women were a bit leery of him; there was something somewhat strange that no one could put a finger on. He felt the pulling away, and I know it hurt.

Whenever he drove by, he'd honk, or I'd wave. Occasionally we'd have a quick chat—he knew my sweetie worked on helicopters in Abu Dhabi.

One morning he phoned me and said, "I could really use some help. Would you stop in on your morning walk?"

I did. He told me he'd been on a two-week drunken binge—blacked out most of the time—and knew he had to get to a detox in the city. Would I take him?

We began the asinine phone call routine with government which had a big, expensive, f-king program for quitting drinking, and there was only an answering machine with a message that said they *would not take long-distance phone calls!*

I left a scathing message and called the Salvation Army. They were like angels. They told us not to worry about a thing—just get him to the detox center, and all would be arranged. They told me to let him clean up his home if that was necessary to him.

"Why?" I asked.

"Because most people know they want to come home to no evidence."

They were right. He needed an hour to clean up his home.

On the trip to the city, I learned that this man managed his life with alcohol. He told me he lived largely in the blackout state! No wonder women found his conversations slightly weird.

He never hurt a soul, and thankfully he somehow managed to work, save lives, and drive in this state of alcohol induced amnesia without harming himself or others.

He left the island after treatment, went on to become an alcohol and drug counselor, and ended up working for a group of First Nations in the North. When he finished his contract with the government agency, on the morning he was to catch his transport out, he was found so inebriated he could neither talk nor move.

Is that the kind of life that vet deserved?

When I see what you have done and when I consider what you have done for others, you have earned a *Gold* Star Metal on this side of war.

Congratulations for both the Bronze and the Gold Stars, my friend.

To use a concept of Thich Nhat Hanh, I want to "hold you home." There is no greater love. It's what you did for your buddies.

04/24/2012 at 01:18
Contoveros says:

It's taken me a while to respond to your heartfelt comment about your experience with your country's Vietnam veteran. It sounds like he used alcohol to deal with the war after the war.

That's what most World War II veterans did who could not own up to having been psychologically scarred. There was too much stigma to being labeled with "shell shock" or "battle fatigue." Still is, but not as much, thanks to the studies done and a slight change in the culture.

Less than 20 percent of veterans sought help for PTSD from the Vietnam War. The percentage is about the same for Iraqi vets, about 17 percent, but increases to 28 percent for a second deployment. There are no studies for third and fourth deployments.

What you offered that young man is all that most veterans seem to want: someone to understand that war claims more casualties than those left behind in the fields of combat.

I thank you for offering that understanding for this Yankee veteran.

Thanks also for that other Thich Nhat Hahn concept to "hold you home." Michael J.

04/24/2012 at 03:46
Souldipper says:

Those percentages are too low. If I knew then what I've come to understand from you, I would have been able to be of better support.

Fear keeps people away when it seems the vet really needs to be seen, heard, and loved.

I'm so glad you have been able to seek help and be such a resource.

04/13/2012 at 00:12
Peaceful Presence Living says:

Thank you for serving, for keeping alive to the best of your ability those around you. Such horror and loss, pain and suffering, and yet you've pulled yourself out of hell, and now use your genuineness and your honest look at life to serve others. You've been doing service work, it sounds like, forever; the expression of that workboat looks different. Maybe the shoulders you stand on are saying thank you. Thank you for being who you are and doing what you do. Your efforts show and are felt; I know they have affected me. Your writing touches many and helps pull us out of our own yells of the moment. Thank you!

04/13/2012 at 02:59
Contoveros says:

I feel safe here to tell stories I was too afraid to look at while they were still raw and unprocessed.

I owe a great deal to people like you who open your door so wide that all feel comfort glowing from the warmth within.

I can't recall the number of firefights we had, but I do remember each time someone was wounded. Four times in six months. Six months was the length of rotation for officers in the field (front line for those still thinking World Wars I and II). I later served in a base camp that had been over-run by the Viet Cong long before my arrival. The most devastating inci-dent occurred to an officer, another first lieutenant, with only a few days left before his DEROS (Date of Expected Return from Overseas). A bunch of kids were playing near some debris which included a shell of some size. It was in an area we called an "ammo dump." It's unclear if the child gave the shell to the soldier to hurt him or if the American took it away to keep harm from befalling on the kid.

The shell blew up, severing one of the arms of the lieutenant.

I never saw or heard anything more about him. He was scheduled to leave that same week. I departed from Vietnam just about two weeks after this incident.

I often wondered, however, how and why someone so close to being safe and sound at home could suffer something like this?

Then I heard of a Vietnamese monk who counseled veterans of the war in his country, and it helped change the way I looked at my tour of duty:

> "We who have touched war have a duty to bring the
> truth about war to those who have not had a direct
> experience of it. We are the light at the tip of the candle.

It is really hot, but it has the power of shining and illuminating. If we practice mindfulness, we will know how to look deeply into the nature of war and, with our insight, wake people up so that together we can avoid repeating the same horrors again and again."

—Thich Nhat Hanh, *Love in Action: Writings on Nonviolent Social Change*

Well, come on all of you, big strong men,

Uncle Sam needs your help again.

He's got himself in a terrible jam

Way down yonder in Vietnam

So put down your books and pick up a gun,

We're gonna have a whole lotta fun.

And it's one, two, three,

What are we fighting for?

Don't ask me, I don't give a damn,

Next stop is Vietnam.

And it's five, six, seven,

Open up the pearly gates,

Well, there ain't no time to wonder why,

Whoopee! We're all gonna die.

—Country Joe and the Fish

PTSD REFRAIN: "WE GOTTA GET OUT OF THIS PLACE"

I heard very little music when I was in the army. We had no radios in boot camp or in Advanced Individual Training. I spent six months in Fort Benning pushing up half of the red clay of Georgia while attending Officer Candidate School. Throw in another three to four weeks for jump school, and you'll get some idea of how deprived I was of listening to music and news of the world around me.

I wanted to cry when I first heard the Beatles sing "Hey Jude." The station I listened to was an oldies station, one noted for playing older songs from the '50s and early '60s. And there I was in Fort Dix, New Jersey, having gone AWOL to visit my nearby Philadelphia, Pennsylvania, home for a lonely weekend. I had not been home for nearly six months, and when I got shipped from basic to the New Jersey fort, I didn't know I needed a pass. I could have gotten a disciplinary sanction, called an Article 15, if the company commander hadn't shown some compassion for me and let it slide.

SECRET CLEARANCE AND MUGGING OF FATHER

I told the captain that I had been kept behind in Fort Bragg, North Carolina, because of a "secret clearance" the army was conducting for my eventual entrance into the OCS. It was the first time I was away from home. And during that time, I learned my father had been mugged and would soon move out of our working-class neighborhood, called Brewerytown.

Well, there I was, sitting in the bus station of Fort Dix, having just returned on a Sunday night. I held a transistor radio to my ear. I had taken the radio from my home and was listening to the oldies when I heard the Beatles sing that mournful song. "Hey Jude" struck a chord inside of me. It went straight to my heart, and I couldn't suppress the tears that begun to form.

OK, I admit it. I shed tears back then, and I didn't give a shit.

Who wouldn't after taking in such lyrics as these?

And anytime you feel the pain, hey Jude, refrain
Don't carry the world upon your shoulders
For well you know that it's a fool who plays it cool
By making his world a little colder…

I cried for my youth. Yeah, I cried for what I had missed being forced to grow up in the army, giving up the days, weeks, and months that others of my age had been given to experiment and explore back home, trying to find themselves. Music, which was a big part of my life, had been taken away from me. Songs had come and gone without my knowledge. "Hey Jude" was one of 'em, I thought, and I missed being young, being, I don't know, more carefree and not concerned about possibly going to war.

Well, I learned later the song was not an oldie, but something inside of me had to make an adjustment. I wasn't the same person I had been before being drafted into the army. I was becoming a soldier, a man who could shoot with the best of the sharpshooters and take pain without bitching or complaining.

Who was it that said it better than I could ever say it?

"I reasoned like a child," the holy man said. "When I became a man, I put the ways of childhood behind me. When I became a man, I gave up childish ways."

⋏　⋏　⋏

I heard no music while humping the bush. All radios were banned, with the exception of that large one the radioman carried on his back for use in the field.

Some music was played in the base camp, but much of it was a form of country and western music which I had not developed a taste for, unless it was Hank Williams or Eddie Arnold singing. My mother had exposed me to those legendary singers, and I don't think anyone has ever come close to replacing them.

I lived for music for two years of my life, when we sang "street corner" harmony in the old neighborhood. I was a damn good baritone but relinquished that position for one of my best friends when we formed a quintet and needed a bass. I was never a good bass, but harmony is harmony, and blending one's voice with another is heavenly.

Our group practiced, and after a while, we caught the attention of a dance-music director. We appeared on a local television program and were damn good, if I do say so myself. Our lead singer was the best, and he would eventually go on to record with other groups in the years to come.

There were two songs that left a lasting impression on me while serving in Vietnam. They dealt with leaving the war-torn country and coming back home. I'll never forget them and, if I have my way, I'll have them played during my cremation services when I pass on.

At the top of the list is the one by Peter, Paul and Mary called "Jet Plane":

I'm leaving on a jet plane.
Don't know when I'll be back again.

That's all young soldiers had to hear to sing along and visualize themselves taking off on the next flight home. Today I can't help but sing along whenever I hear that song. I know it deals with love and leaving home, but no song captured my feelings for returning home better than that one.

The next was a close second, and it, too, moves me whenever I hear it played on television oldies revival programs.

We gotta get out of this place
If it's the last thing we ever do.
We gotta get out of this place
'Cause girl, there's a better life
For me and you.

Thank God for The Animals. They helped many a grunt get through another day and another night, just chanting that refrain over and over.

Well, that brings us to more recent history and a song a friend of mine introduced me to following a deep meditation. "Still in Saigon" is about the Vietnam War and about the mindset that many of us who got marked in combat suffer from years later.

I wrote the following for my blog and can't help but feel the songwriter had fought in combat in some previous life in order for him to have captured a soldier's lament like he did.

Above all, Vietnam was a war that asked everything of a few and nothing of most in America.

—Myra MacPherson

NEED NOT BATTLE
TO UNDERSTAND
WAR HORRORS

https://contoveros.com/2012/04/06/
need-not-battle-to-understand-war-horrors/

When I heard the song "Still in Saigon" the other day, I could have sworn a Vietnam veteran had written about his flashbacks and a need to process what was unprocessed as a young man.

Little did I know that the writer had never set foot in Southeast Asia, let alone put on a uniform and served in the military. That got me wondering about the performing arts and how someone who never experienced war could capture its long-term effects on those who faced combat.

The song was written in 1981 and made popular a year later when performed by the Charlie Daniels Band. The songwriter, Dan Daley, was a journalist and author who generally wrote about the music industry. His soldier protagonist in this song recalls the war during the summer months when it rains and when he hears certain aircraft flying nearby, despite having been discharged from the military and having served in Vietnam ten years earlier.

I took notice of the lyrics because I, too, left in 1971. But my flashbacks did not reach a crescendo until some twenty-five years later, when I sought help for anger management and years later for what I learned is the correct diagnosis, PTSD. (I've dropped the term "disorder" and refer to it as "post-traumatic stress" because of the stigma attached to it.)

The song captures the feeling many veterans experienced when settling back into civilian life. They live in the world "back home" but are still in the war zone when certain triggering events and stressful circumstances flare up.

Actor Gregory Peck, who was honored this week by President Barack Obama for his portrayal fifty years ago of Atticus Finch in the movie *To Kill a Mockingbird*, captures a wounded soldier's true mindset in an earlier performance as a television adman in *The Man in the Gray Flannel Suit*. The movie depicts an up-and-coming operative whose thoughts often drift back to Italy ten years earlier and the time he and his generation spent fighting in World War II.

Not all flashbacks are bad, particularly those to the girl he met and left behind in the war-torn country. (He later learns of the child their relationship had resulted in.) Unfortunately, his mind also dredges up incidents from combat, and he finds himself needing to deal with experiences not fully processed back home in peacetime. The war's aftermath affects not only him but also his family, who struggle to understand how the young man had changed into someone at times unrecognizable.

My favorite singer-songwriter Bobby Darin presented us with the essence of war in the movie *Captain Newman, M.D.* The 1960s creator of the songs "Splish Splash" and "Mack the Knife" was nominated for an Academy Award for portraying a serviceman in World War II who watched his entire aircraft crew die when their plane was hit and he survived. He's admitted to a military hospital, where he's treated for shell shock and battle fatigue. Darin fights images of nightmares projected from his subconscious. He cries out, swings at invisible enemies, and wishes he could have died along with the others. In time he appears cured in the movie and is sent back into battle, only to have his death wish granted.

Neither Darin nor Peck ever fought in war. But each understood it and helped noncombatants see its long-term effects. There really are no winners in most, if not all, wars. Ask those who are "Still in Baghdad."

FOUR COMMENTS ON "NEED NOT BATTLE TO UNDERSTAND WAR HORRORS"

04/12/2012 at 06:21
Bob Palumbo says:

Mike, still digging on Bobby Darin, I see. Found a letter the other day you sent me Easter Sunday of '71. You had a "Free Calley" stamp on it that I found amusing. I still tell the story of our triple date—me, you, and Carl Disler somewhere near Fort Polk. Glad to see you're doing well.—Lumbo

04/13/2012 at 03:34
Contoveros says:

Nineteen seventy-one! What a year and what a memory.

Throw in a "Free Calley" stamp to boot. Little did we know then about what actually had transpired in the Twenty-Third Division known as the "American."

The killing of seventeen innocent Afghanistan civilians by a rogue US sergeant palls in comparison.

Let's not forget Fort Polk, Louisiana, which some called the "armpit of the army." It was a jumping off point for me to Vietnam and for Carl Disler to return to the states. You had already served one tour there and got shrapnel that you carried with you for the next, I don't know, forty years or so?

Why were we among the only few drafted? There were many others in our old neighborhood, but how did those in our age bracket avoid it? In a way, I feel sorry for them. They may have missed out on an experience that taught some of the greatest lessons about truly living, as did Bobby Darin who truly lived the short thirty-some-odd years he was with us. I have written four articles about him—my teenage idol—including this one.

Good to hear from you Bob.

See you around soon!

Michael J.

04/09/2012 at 21:52
Raven says:

Contoveros (what does that word mean?), I, a sixty-five-year-old woman who has definitely not been to war, can tell you that I have felt what many have felt while at war. In Western society, we are taught not to feel. It is "sissified"…to feel, that is. But it is only when one can feel that we can develop true compassion for others. And I mean feel deeply.

So much of who we are is about what we can feel. With me, it was a sort of "ask and you shall receive." When we are willing to give up our own feelings and receive the feelings of others, we truly can learn of others and develop compassion and empathy. I know that we have spoken of this before.

This was a really good piece. I hope that it gets a wide readership and that people have one of those "aha" moments when they read it.

04/11/2012 at 03:08
Contoveros says:

My dear Raven,

"Contoveros" was the name my father brought with him from Greece until it got shortened to "Contos" by workers in Ellis Island, New York. (Or was it New Jersey?)

It has been translated by some to mean "singer" or "teller of truth."

I heard somewhere that 1 percent of the population are empathetic by nature. Only 1 percent of those people act upon their empathy by performing random acts of kindness and compassion. I see you are among them and can not only "feel" the hardships and sufferings of others but do something about it in your daily life.

Thanks for your understanding and your active support of all veterans.
Michael J.

PART III

VIETNAM WAR RECALLED BY ANOTHER GENERATION

Most veterans who faced combat hardly ever talk about their experiences. Just ask their families. Oh, we'll joke about some things and mention what it was like on R & R. I went to Hawaii, where most married men ended up with their spouses, buying trinkets and spending lost time alone with the ones they loved. Single guys went usually went to Bangkok or Sydney, Australia.

I never told my family about the worst day of my life. Even when my son asked me what it was like to kill an enemy soldier, I never told him about combat or its lasting effect on my soul. He must have learned something from my refusal to talk of the horror of war, and he grew to respect my contribution to our nation and the contributions of others like me who placed themselves in harm's way.

He wrote the following not too long ago, and I have never been so proud of him for his tribute to his old man and old men everywhere who are forced to forego boyhood for immediate manhood under fire.

Thank you, Nicholas Alexander!

I was proud of the youths who opposed the war in Vietnam because they were my babies.

—Benjamin Spock

MY FAVORITE VETERANS DAY TRIBUTE EVER

[My favorite son, Nick Contos Petrilli,
sent this via Facebook on Veterans Day.]

https://contoveros.com/2014/11/12/my-favorite-veterans-day-tribute-ever/amp/

I want to wish a happy Veterans Day to all veterans. Veterans I know and veterans I don't know alike.

Today is your day to celebrate and be proud of something not a lot of other Americans have/had the balls to do. I thank you all, whether you were in the marines, army, navy, air force, or some other branch of service to our country.

▲　▲　▲

But I would like to thank one man in particular. This man pushed up his draft so he could fight in Vietnam. He was only eighteen or nineteen at the time (can't remember). This man was eventually promoted to the rank of first lieutenant. At the time, the lifespan of a first lieutenant in the war zone he was in was only sixteen minutes.

He led his own platoon. None of his troops were killed.

I am very proud of this man and his accomplishments.

This man, however, is the craziest (by "crazy," I mean "borderline insane"), weirdest, most loving, caring, and amazing man I've had the pleasure of knowing. This man is my father, 1st Lt. Michael J. Contos (aka Contoveros).

▲   ▲   ▲

I am extremely proud to call this man my father. I have looked up to this man all my life. He's kept me out of (most) trouble.

He will always be there for me. He will always defend me.

Yeah, sure, we get on each other's nerves, and sometimes I have to keep him out of trouble, but we love each other to death. And that's the God's honest truth.

So here it is, Dad. Happy Veterans Day, you old fart.

Hahaha, I love you, Dad. I always will, no matter what.

Vietnam was what we had instead of happy childhoods.

—Michael Herr

TIME TRAVELING WITH
A GRIZZLY OLD VET

While we're talking about Veterans Day acknowledgments, I'd like to share one that I wrote on the fortieth anniversary of my combat experience in Vietnam. I was wondering what it would be like to get into a time machine and go back to when I was a young man in the army after being drafted and trained as a soldier to kill another in the name of my country.

I might have been an acting corporal stationed at Fort Dix, New Jersey, or a recruit given the rank of Specialist 5 (Spec-5) to attend Officers Candidates School. Or maybe I was the brand-new officer, a second lieutenant filled with spit and polish and awaiting my turn to lead men into a battle I believed my country needed me to engage in.

Now, you gotta use your imagination. I know of no time travelers who were ever permitted to come into contact with their younger selves, let alone talk to 'em. But for this moment, just suspend your judgment. Join with me as if you're a grizzly old vet who has accumulated a little wisdom while living on this good earth.

Better yet, try to visualize yourself going back to a time when you could have used some sound advice about something important to you way back when. Perhaps it had to do with not marrying that no-good so-and-so or taking the job that paid you less but made you happier.

Now come along with me as I speak to that nineteen- or twenty-year-old who is about to go to war. He'll eventually complete jump school, get toughened up as he gets his wings as a parachutist, and learn the lay of the land while undergoing jungle training in Panama.

Better yet, join me as I speak to a boy who returned home from the war but could never truly find himself until now.

There is the guilt all soldiers feel for having broken the taboo against killing, a guilt as old as war itself. Add to this the soldier's sense of shame for having fought in actions that resulted, indirectly or directly, in the deaths of civilians. Then pile on top of that an attitude of social opprobrium, an attitude that made the fighting man feel personally morally responsible for the war, and you get your proverbial walking time bomb.

—Philip Caputo

WAR IS NEVER THE ANSWER: FROM A VET ON 11-11-11

https://contoveros.com/2011/11/02/
war-is-never-the-answer-11-11-11/

On this Veterans Day 2011, what would you tell yourself if you could go back in time and greet that young man recently returned home from the war?

War is never the answer but is only a failure on all sides to reach the right solution. That's my feeling about war today.

I would tell that twenty-two-year-old not to be angry at an enemy his country had demonized today, for tomorrow that country may become a trading partner with us. Also that the enemies' beliefs may one day become our beliefs, particularly if we seek enlightenment within, where his future spiritual teachers will tell all of us to look.

Don't be mad at or hold a grudge against those who avoided what you simply called "doing your duty." They, too, were afraid to face war and in not going to war because they questioned whether they were man enough to give their lives for another…even if that "other" was a Jew or gentile, a white or Black man, or an Irishman or a Greek man who became your buddy in the bush.

They will never know how you came truly alive when you faced the real possibility of death. How you survived on nothing but your wits, your cunning, and the compassion for your fellow men whose lives depended on your doing the right thing, doing your duty even if it meant bringing injury to yourself to help the members of your squad or platoon.

You cared nothing about an economic system back home that might one day disintegrate from the greed crushing down from the top or whether one fundamentalist group would seek to destroy another in the name of an Allah, a Jesus, or a Jehovah.

Your purpose this Veterans Day 2011 is to reaffirm your commitment to your fellow man, the one you looked after and would have given your life to safeguard. He is as close to you today as he was years ago, and you can see him in the faces of every man, woman, and child who wants no more from life than what you did when you took up your rifle and offered to protect everyone: to end suffering and to attain happiness.

Put down your weapon, Michael J.
Study war no more.

VIETNAM WAR VET
RECALLS BATTLE JOURNEY

https://contoveros.com/2012/05/16/
vietnam-veteran-recalls-war-for-student/

Dealing with the Vietnam War becomes a little easier each time I write about it. I desensitize myself and now see my actions as separate from the emotions I felt while a young soldier and the guilt many veterans, like me, imposed on ourselves while readjusting to civilian life. It's helpful when a high school student asks questions, and you try to be honest and direct.

The following is a veteran's look at the war years after he replaced his M16 rifle with college textbooks in a world brighter than the one he left behind. You can call it the second in a series of articles on Vietnam. (See first article at "Questions and Answers on Vietnam War" in chapter 5.) I'll call it an exercise in atonement and redemption.

▲   ▲   ▲

"Hey, my name is Matan Baron, and I am a senior at Tenafly High School in New Jersey. I have been asked by my teacher to interview war veterans, and after reading your blog, I wanted to ask you if you would be willing to answer a few questions about being a part of the Vietnam War. I would really appreciate it, thank you very much.

"Before I state my questions, I just wanted to tell you how grateful I am for you taking your time to answer them. I really appreciate it. Tenafly is about fifteen minutes away from New York City and about thirty minutes from Newark. Here are my questions."—Matan

How was your life before the war?

I was lost and adrift with no real direction or purpose in life until I got drafted into the US Army. And just as I thought things couldn't get any worse, they did!

I'm only kidding. Partially, that is. I had graduated from high school two years before I was drafted. I worked as a laborer after leaving a better job as a printer because of the hours. I didn't like working the second shift—3:00 p.m.–11:00 p.m.—as a printer. I wanted to socialize more. That also meant getting into more trouble by experimenting with some psychedelic stuff that I'd rather not discuss even after all these years. (For more, see a history on Dr. Timothy Leary, a Harvard professor who introduced our generation to "trips" to places you'd not find on a map, in his favorite consciousness-raising book, *The Tibetan Book of the Dead.*)

I had dated but had no special girl, although I always thought I'd end up marrying the girl I had gone steady with on and off for three years. I was devastated when I heard that she had gotten pregnant and was getting married while I was in my second year of a three-year army hitch.

My favorite activities included singing in a doo-wop group, five guys who harmonized on the street corner and even appeared on a rock and roll television show. I could dance and do a mean split while doing something called the "mashed potatoes." I enjoyed driving my own car, a ten-year-old 1957 Chevy, which had bad brakes and even worse gas mileage. (I loved that car. I paid all of $300 to buy it from my barber.)

Why did you join the war (unless you got drafted)?

I had "pushed up" my draft and then asked to enter the military two weeks later to go to boot camp with one of my friends with whom I sang. Going to Canada was not an option, as it was for some, mostly college-educated fellows who knew more about politics than I did at age nineteen. I felt serving in the army was simply doing my duty.

How was your experience in the training camp?

Boot camp was not difficult. It got easier once I got over the initial shock of losing all my hair and doing push-ups every time the drill sergeant looked my way and ordered me "give [him] twenty." I always had pretty good upper-body strength, so it wasn't too bad.

One of the most trying events occurred two days after I was drafted on June 3, 1968. Presidential candidate Bobby Kennedy was shot and killed June 6, 1968, and I wanted to stop marching and playing soldier long enough to mourn his death but could not. The toughest thing about being away from home for the first time was learning that sometimes you have to keep your emotions in check until you can process them in private.

I was in good physical shape, despite smoking cigarettes from age twelve, and I didn't mind the two months of a structured lifestyle. The worst part, however, was the loss of privacy when using the latrine. There ain't no stalls in the bathroom/shower room, and when you got to go, you got to go with four or five guys all going at the same time.

Tell me about your experience in the war, the battles, and such.

This is something few if any combat veterans like to talk about because of the stress that recalling these events stirs up.

My first day in the combat zone, I saw a member of my new platoon refuse to fight anymore and then deck our company commander with a roundhouse blow to the chin when the captain ordered him to man up and go into the field.

The first person killed in my company was an officer, a lieutenant, one of only three in the company. There was an urban legend that the life expectancy of a second lieutenant dropped off by a helicopter into a "hot LZ," that is, a landing zone under fire by the enemy, was sixteen minutes.

I didn't know this when my oldest brother convinced me to go to OCS and earn a commission as a lieutenant; I got sent to Vietnam less than a year after graduating from Officer Candidate School. (Thank you, Brother George!)

Friendly fire took its toll on two soldiers from the Second Platoon. They put out a trip wire to a Claymore mine and forgot where it was, getting killed as they walked into it.

My medic wrapped his foot with bandages, laced up his boot, and shot himself with a .45 to get out of the field.

Five guys in my platoon were wounded when a mortar shell from our side fell on them.

A lieutenant who had chased Vietnamese kids away from playing with a shell along the perimeter of an ammo dump lost an arm when it exploded, this happening only two days before he was to leave Vietnam.

We used no fixed bayonets. There was no hand-to-hand combat. The only time we saw the enemy was when we glimpsed him in triple-canopy jungle or walked up to his encampment and he fled with us firing in his direction. We would not know if we hit anyone until we came across a body.

I still loathe the battalion commander who wanted a higher body count for his promotion from lieutenant colonel to a higher rank as a "full bird" colonel.

Lieutenant Colonel Salucci was the only officer I knew whose own men fragged him, but he survived when the hand grenade couldn't penetrate the sandbags covering his bunker.

How did the war affect your life? How was it to come back home?

I tried to put Vietnam behind me and never talk about it, even with veterans who formed a vets' club at the community college I attended right out of the service.

Going to school less than two weeks after leaving Vietnam gave me serious culture shock. I was not used to guys with such long hair and the girls who swooned over them or to hugging everyone at sensitivity meetings in college introductory sessions. (I was afraid I'd hit someone if they tried to hug me. Not that there's anything wrong with it, but my head was "still in Saigon," as the Charlie Daniels Band sang. I wasn't ready for any touchy-feely contact.)

I slept in no underwear my first year back. We wore none so our uniforms could dry more quickly from the rainy season, streams we forged, and rice paddies we sometimes got soaked in. I was quick to awaken and take action when someone roused me from sleep.

I had nightmares. I'd get flashbacks whenever I heard a helicopter fly above me. I mistrusted authority figures and knew I'd suffer trauma the rest of my life while voting for the Democratic Party. (I'm only joking about my mistrust of authority, not about the Democrats!)

I used reverse psychology on myself, saying that I felt that the war was a failure, and I needed so badly to succeed in civilian life. I excelled at the community college, getting enough credits to transfer to a university and get a BA in three years and an MA a year later. That's three degrees in four years, including the associate's degree, as I crammed all my studies into the forty-eight months the GI Bill was willing to support me for.

Military life and serving our country in time of war was invaluable to me. I wouldn't pass it up for all the money in the world, but you couldn't pay me enough to do it again.

Do you keep in touch with any of the people you fought with?

No. I've spoken by phone to the other lieutenant I served with during my 1970–71 tour. He found God outside Arkadelphia, Arkansas, and I told him that I was still hot on His trail. I made a promise to visit the Virginia town that gave us the third member of our lieutenants' club, the one that was killed by sniper fire, but I have yet to cross it off my bucket list of things to do.

Who knows? Maybe this exercise will inspire me to take action.

What are your best and worst memories from the war?

A mortar platoon honored me with a twenty-one-gun salute when I left the base camp my last day in the combat zone of Vietnam. I had to hold in my emotions and have only recently been able to cherish that moment after years of deep reflections.

The deep reflections, however, dealt mostly with the negative side of war, when soldiers were injured or killed, and I realized decades later that we might have been on the wrong side of history. The Vietnamese people wanted independence from both foreign countries—France and the United States—but our leaders did not understand that until we agreed to be trading partners with them thirty years after the fall of Saigon and the end of the war.

My worst day was when I called for mortar fire to fall on the enemy and the fire fell on the platoon I was leading, injuring five men, one of whom was seeing combat for the first time that day. I'll never forget the pain and anguish my mistake put him and the others through. I'll live with it the rest of my life and hope we never have to go to war like this again.

Respectfully submitted,
Michael J. Contos,
Veteran, first lieutenant, US Army Infantry, serving in Chu Lai and Cu Chi, the former Republic of South Vietnam

---

In war, there are no unwounded soldiers.

—José Narosky

WORST DAY OF MY LIFE LASTED ALL MY LIFE

I felt, or rather sensed, danger whenever I had to lead my platoon into and across a waterway. We'd waded through them before with nary a mishap, save for leeches that we'd have to burn off clinging to our bodies. You had to be very gentle with any of the leeches that got too close to your genitals. Thank God I never had to drop my drawers to burn one.

None of the squad members I was with ever found out what was on the other side of the last waterway we were ordered to cross on the worst day of my life. I called for mortar fire for a section directly across from where we were to traverse. A sergeant with some ten years in the army was in charge of the mortar platoon, somewhere closer to, or perhaps even in, our secured base camp. His men did not accompany us to the field. I spoke to him about my suspicions of something not feeling right. Heavy artillery fire had rained onto that area a day earlier. Somebody somewhere must have determined there was an earlier danger and called in the fire. Hell, a few of those rounds nearly hit us!

I plotted the coordinates for where I wanted mortars to be dropped. Taking the handheld black radio communicator from my operator's backpack, I requested two rounds fired.

There was a silence for several long moments, and then I heard sounds in the distance. The shells had fallen way off the target. They were well beyond the location had I requested them to hit.

I asked the mortar platoon to step back the next shots as I patiently waited with one of the two squads in the platoon. We had between eight and ten men that day. Somehow it seemed we were always under strength but did what we were ordered to do despite our numbers. I would rotate between the two squads, and I remember having accompanied this squad the night before. Looking back, I can't recall exactly where the other squad had been, but we had taken the lead for the platoon and for the three platoons of our company on this field mission.

Those of us waiting near the river looked in the direction where the rounds went off. I thought they were half a kilometer away from us.

The next series of rounds landed. I couldn't determine any difference from the rounds that had fallen first. I ordered another step back, hoping it would bring the missiles closer to the other side of the river, the side where we were to reconnoiter and secure.

They fell wide again, so I requested another step back, and another, to bring carnage to an enemy I believed was waiting for us.

A round struck mere feet from where I had been clutching the radio receiver. The noise was so tremendous it contributed to the hearing loss I developed while in Vietnam. I could never prove whether the loss was due to this incident or from artillery being fired from positions we'd patrolled while on guard duty later.

When I could make out sounds, I head men groaning. One young man, barely nineteen years old and in the field for the very first time, lay just a few feet away from me. I don't know whether he had lost his kneecap, but he was in severe pain. I later noticed drops of liquid on my uniform and realized his blood had sprayed on me as his leg was struck.

He screamed in agony, crying hysterically from the pain. His voice drowned out by the less shrill voices of four others who got hit by the explosion of the mortar round, including the squad leader, a sergeant who aided the wounded despite his own injuries.

I immediately called for a medevac, providing the necessary information for a rescue mission. I could hardly hear myself talk as the injured private screamed more and more loudly.

"You're going to be OK," I said, removing the radio receiver from my ear and leaning toward the young man, trying to determine the severity of his wound. "I called for help, and they're on their way."

Something almost miraculous occurred. He stopped crying. That boy just out of Advanced Individual Training was being addressed by his superior officer. He showed his bravery by overcoming his pain as we made eye contact, and he listened intently to what I said.

I continued talking to him as I waited for the helicopter crew to reply over the "horn." As soon as someone spoke, I broke eye contact with the private and spoke into the receiver. I had to give the pilot my undivided attention and help guide him to us.

The wounded soldier cried out, wailing like he had sobbed moments before our communing together. He carried on and on as I stayed with the chopper crew via the radio. As soon as I turned back to the young man and spoke to him, he stopped crying. I'd later think of this moment as a parent, investigating the discomfort of a baby who stops their focus on an irritation while their attention is drawn to a kind voice seeking to alleviate their suffering and bring calm to their life.

I realized that the infantryman could focus less on his fears and pain and more on the hopes his LT could offer to him. I have no idea what I said, but whatever it was, he remained calm and more peaceful, sobbing here and there as the pain became more acute but not giving in to the frenzied feeling of utter loss. I like to think I kept this fellow from going into shock, that I was able to soothe him a little bit after being responsible for the pain he suffered to begin with…

▲   ▲   ▲

Looking back over years of successes and failures I'd eventually experience, I see that moment as the worst day of my life. Try as I might, I can't recall any details about the explosion. I remember the next-to-last round going off in the distance. I heard it first and then saw a plume of smoke rise from the treetops. To my mind and eyesight, it appeared a long distance across the river where we had to cross. I wanted to hit the opposite side of the river, so I called in another round.

There must have been a deafening sound as the round hit within several meters of where I sat with the radio near my ear. I wasn't looking toward the rear or to the side but to the front, where I had hoped the firepower would cause most of its damage.

I often visualized a white light exploding as I tried to best to see the devastation. No, I don't have a recall of the actual blast that had occurred, but sometimes I could swear that I felt a flash somewhere around me. I can't say more without sounding a little crazy.

I don't remember the sound either. I heard plenty of bombs go off. Why, just the day before, I'd felt the ground shake and crumble when an artillery shell fell close to my site. If you've ever experienced an earthquake, increase the rumbling tenfold: then you'd know what my men and I went through from the friendly fire.

A Blow to the Senses

My ears are still paying a price for the explosions I was exposed to in combat and during guard duty for an artillery gun that fired right next to the bunker where I was keeping watch. I got a 10 percent disability for my hearing loss.

I don't really know when the loud noises took their toll on me. It could have been that day the mortar round fell on my platoon's location.

Debris from the shell exploding from the ground must have struck me. Blood from a nearby private splattered onto one of my pant legs. But I didn't feel it or notice anything until later, when I experienced a stinging sensation in spots along my leg and saw the stain of blood on the pants of my uniform.

I remember what the friendly fire explosion tasted like. There was a metallic taste that I had felt some twenty-four hours earlier. I noticed what I can only call a metallic flavor in my mouth. Although my throat had gone dry, I tasted something akin to what a Lincoln-head penny tasted like if you ever got one of those germ-coated coins in your mouth.

To be perfectly honest, I didn't know what had happened at first. I did notice some smoke and knew something was wrong. I thought it was the enemy firing from across the river. Nothing happened immediately after the blast. There was no follow-up by the Viet Cong nor return fire from our side. The silence was eerie.

But it didn't last long, as I began to hear screams and groans from the men that had been wounded. I believe that at least five men got hit. As I just said, the one was within feet of my position, but I didn't notice until I turned toward his direction to discover what had happened. I didn't know, and it took forever for my mind to begin to register in slow motion what was happening.

"My leg, my leg!" the young soldier cried as I looked toward the blackened blood that seem to be pouring out of a part of his knee. I went to him and, bending down, I tried to get a better look at the leg. He screamed even more loudly when I touched his clothes.

I backed up slightly and called for my radio operator. By this time men were running toward me, telling me of others who had gotten hit in the small area where we had come to rest. I put a call out to my captain, and soon I was in contact with a helicopter crew. The group landed and helped all of the wounded onto the chopper and took them for medical help in the rear.

I never learned what had happened to the men. All survived, however, and I am grateful for that blessing.

▲   ▲   ▲

Why am I unable to remember many details of the worst moment of my life? What happened to me to block out all recall? I put those questions to an expert dealing with posttraumatic stress disorder, Dr. Howard Cohen. A psychologist who has been treating veterans with PTSD for some thirty years, he told me that it was not unusual for someone to simply forget the incident. He told me that the PTSD had "anesthetized" that moment, numbing all emotions connected with the explosion. I might not be able to recall the details even under hypnosis, which I never plan to seek. There are some things, some traumas, best left undisturbed.

Maybe that's why most combat soldiers don't like to talk about their combat. Sometimes it is best to simply let it be.

Please don't ask 'em to relive those memories.

Sometime they'll give a war, and nobody will come.

—Carl Sandburg

BEST DAY OF MY LIFE: A TWENTY-ONE- GUN BLASTOFF

How many people do you know who have ever gotten a twenty-one-gun salute? I'm talking about while they're still alive, not when they've passed on and a military honor guard helps to usher them to the next life.

The salute came on my last day in the combat zone. It was something I had initially dismissed. I believed I did not deserve the honor, and I minimized it for most of my life afterward. If the troops I commanded outside Cu Chi during the second half of my tour in Vietnam had known of my earlier blunder, they would never have seen me off with such flair. Now I see that it was a yin-yang type of action. Vietnam would always carry the memories of my worst day, and the salute on the base camp turned out to be one of my best days ever!

Why do we focus on the bad and tend to overlook the good? Calling friendly fire on my troops haunted me all of my life. All I recall about serving in the war since that painful day is tainted by that memory. It imprinted the mark of failure in me, and it has taken four decades for me to look back and see the false reality I had created. I created a memory based on immaturity, negative emotions, and that feeling of victimization that has echoed through the years as "woe is me."

I can now look that incident dead in its eye and see it for what it really was: an accident. I was twenty years old when commissioned, twenty-one when given command of an infantry platoon. Who the hell has accumulated any wisdom at that age?

▲　▲　▲

Don't get me wrong. I'm no sage of old, divining the true meanings of life. I've learned I know less today than I ever knew and that I need the help of my friends to give me better insight into my true being, my relationship to and with the world.

What's this have to do with seeing my past by seeing my self-created memories? It's a simple thing called karma, or the good and bad energy from previous thoughts and actions. How else can I explain these circumstances except through this notion of good and bad acts from previous thoughts and actions affecting the present stream of life? More importantly, what action is the right action for me to take as my karma arises? As my Buddhist friends say, "When causes and conditions are ripe, things will reveal themselves." Do I do anything different this time around, under this condition, or should I let these same conditions continue without a break in the flow or a change in the narrative or my understanding of the events?

I don't know why fate placed me in charge of a mortar platoon when my old division, the Twenty-Fifth Infantry Division, conducted a "stand down" and I was reassigned further north in Vietnam. The Twenty-Fifth stopped all missions outside of Saigon, particularly in the area of Chu Lai, where my battalion operated. All troops with "time in" or with tours about to finish within four weeks were given an early leave and got sent home. I had a little more than half a tour completed, some six months in country, and the army reassigned me to a rear position at a base camp that was somewhat secure but had once been overrun by the Viet Cong.

I ended up in the Twenty-Third Infantry Division, the one Lt. William Calley had made infamous some years earlier when he permitted his platoon to wreak havoc on the village of My Lai.

My worst day was entangled with a mortar platoon someone else commanded. My best was with a mortar platoon I commanded. Why have I not been able to see and understand this before? Why could I not see the almost mystical balancing out of my life? Why has it fallen into place just as I needed such a healing?

"My karma has ripened." Causes and conditions from a long life of actions have finally come together, and *wham!* I can see clearly now for the first time ever. This was what Japanese Buddhists call a "satori," or an awakening.

I did very little while serving in the base camp. I made no friends and stayed away from any involvement with others. It was not as difficult as it might sound. As an officer, I segregated myself from the rest of the troops. I slept alone, sleeping in a small bunker, with just enough room for a cot and one bookshelf to fit books I'd pick up for life outside Vietnam. (Plato's *Republic* and several Isaac Asimov Foundation books come to mind.)

I ate in a mess hall at a small table with other junior officers, most of whom I had little or no interest in, save for the fellow who later lost his arm when taking away an unexploded shell from one of the Vietnamese children playing outside the base camp. I can't remember his name or recall what we had in common except that he gave me a tour of the camp and welcomed me there.

My job was to instill discipline while permitting those who knew their jobs to continue without my interference. I served as pay officer for camp one time, coming up short but not reporting it to anyone who might see how inefficient I was with money. (I still am.) I short-changed myself some forty dollars but said not a word until now.

There were two squads that I was placed in charge of. One squad consisted mostly of potheads, those that seemed to get high but could function without too much effort as long as they had some packages from home with goodies to munch on. I never bought into the ban on marijuana. I figured a soldier could drink on his time off as long as his habit didn't interfere with his job. I didn't discriminate against those who smoked, and I never had cause to bring the hammer down on someone who screwed up.

Until one day, when a scrawny little private mouthed off and refused to follow orders of a platoon sergeant who had just joined us. I don't even remember what issue had been raised or what commands may have been ignored. I believe it had more to do with cleaning the workstation than any type of dereliction of duty. I suspected this private of getting high a lot. In fact, I suspected—and others partially confirmed—that most, if not all, members of the first squad of which I was in charge smoked grass. As I said, I didn't care, if I never saw it—my version of "don't ask, don't tell." That squad provided a supporting role to the more technologically gifted squad that really controlled the big guns, the large mortar weapons. Like me, that latter squad stayed sober day in and day out, never knowing when they'd be called on to fire the guns in support of fellow soldiers outside the base or, on rare occasions, in defense of the base.

The sergeant whose order the private ignored was a lean and mean African American who reminded me of Lou Gossett Jr.'s character in *An Officer and a Gentleman*. He expected troops to be present at the job and get started when he ordered them to work. This private had flouted his authority more than once, and when this incident was brought to my attention, I acted immediately. I ordered the private off the base camp and into an infantry platoon to hump the boonies, living on C rations in the field for two weeks straight before returning to camp. The enemy had a better chance of shooting you in the field than in the rear.

I took the action to show support for the sergeant but also to send a message to that private and to all others: "We are at war, motherfuckers. You can't decide which order to follow or not to follow. You must act with precision when someone who knows more than you orders you to act. Your life and the lives of others could depend on it."

▲   ▲   ▲

I remember when I pointed my M16 rifle at a private who was too slow in following an order when we were in the bush. We had just come across a tunnel used by the Viet Cong, and I wanted him to secure the entrance and remain there while I led others to look elsewhere. The private had served as my radio operator at an earlier time. We got to know one another well enough to joke and to exchange some pleasantries.

But I kept a distance between us. I'd also do this with some relationships I would develop later on, putting off any intimacy that would reveal any weaknesses. I followed the old adage "familiarity breeds contempt." And in the middle of a war, I didn't want or need someone I was friendly toward to ask why when I ordered them to do something.

"Move your fucking ass," I still remember saying to him. I felt all the eyes of other platoon members on our brief exchange. You never point your weapon at another person unless you plan to use it, and I don't know what I would have done had the soldier not responded in the manner I believed the situation called for. I like to think I would not have fired *on* him, only in his direction. Thank God I never had to find out.

▲   ▲   ▲

I had no problem in ordering the mortar platoon soldier out of the comforts of the base camp and into the field. Hell, I wouldn't have minded going back into the field, proving myself after that disastrous day. There was such a freedom in being in nature, even if you were exposing yourself to being shot. For one thing, you didn't have to bathe. Nor did you need to brush your teeth, comb your hair, or apply deodorant. I had no concern about the so-called niceties of life, and there was something liberating about being with men who cared nothing about the daily grooming chores civilized society demanded of you.

Life had more meaning while walking one path in Vietnam after another. You were providing a service. You were in closer touch with the purpose of life, even if that purpose called on you to take another's life to preserve yours and the lives of the men you served with.

Word of my draconian order to send a man back into the field filtered through the camp. The first sergeant, the highest-ranking noncommissioned officer and one of the most respected, approached me and diplomatically asked me to rescind the order. I wondered why but never voiced the question. We were all soldiers trained to do the same thing. What was wrong with doing it closer to enemy fire rather than further away?

At first I refused. I could not see the big deal people had made out of this. I had actually forgotten about the order when he asked me to reconsider it.

"Only if the platoon sergeant agrees," I finally told the first sergeant, a giant of a man nearly twice my size in height and in girth, not to mention age and senior military knowledge.

The sergeant agreed, and that's exactly how the private was saved from doing hard duty. Even so, I believe the mortar platoon valued me as a leader because I was willing to impose a harsh duty, the lone available brand of justice, on a soldier for his inappropriate behavior. My past deeds surfaced, and I relived them, particularly the two times I was relieved of my command and hurt beyond anything that had ever hurt me before or since. Yes, it all came back.

I never felt as low as I did after bring relieved of my command. That's what the technical process is called when someone sacks you in the military. It happened to me and to the first lieutenant in charge of the Second Platoon. As I mentioned earlier, the Third Platoon leader, Victor Lee Ellinger, was shot and killed by a Viet Cong sniper.

Initially, I became numb as the investigation into his killing was conducted in near-record time. We were at war, remember, and his killing took precedence over other things.

I continued to serve as platoon leader. I remember that someone from the rear had interviewed me. I believe it was a major. He spoke to others, including the career sergeant (also known as a "lifer") who was in charge of the mortar platoon that fired the rounds.

▲   ▲   ▲

A mortar is a small muzzle-loading cannon with a tube that is short in relation to its caliber. It throws projectiles or rounds with a low muzzle velocity at high angles.

I must admit that I knew next to nothing about the weapons except for what I had learned in the brief courses I took in OCS involving the use of artillery and mortars. However, I was expert in map reading and providing coordinates to locations both near and far. I just never fired a cannon myself.

Those who loaded the so-called cannon were interviewed as part of the investigation. Within two or three days, the investigation was completed and the results were made known. I, the first lieutenant, was at fault and was immediately fired upon my return to the rear area from leading my platoon in combat.

▲   ▲   ▲

I remember lying on a canvas cot in a tent in a secure area in a base camp. I was facedown with my head to the side, wishing that I could somehow dig into the hardened earth floor beneath me. I didn't want to live anymore. I wished that I had died when the round struck.

I saw no future for myself. No hope for better days back home with my family and friends. I had invested all of myself into serving my men, and I had fucked up. I had fucked up royally.

And then there came a reprieve. I got called out of the depths of hell and found myself once again before Lieutenant Colonel Salucci, the man I would come to despise and hate more than anyone I would ever know, including the Prosecutorial Judge Guarino.

▲　　▲　　▲

He assigned me to another platoon. One in a different company under his command as battalion leader. He must have seen something good in me. He was giving me another chance to prove myself. I was surprised at how quickly I responded and looked forward to my new command.

I could not let him down. I couldn't fail him again, I said to myself as I took over the new platoon, instilling an esprit de corps that had been sorely lacking. I trained several men to do double duty, that is, serve as medics should the regular one get injured or killed, learn to fire and carry the big M60 machine gun, or be radio operators. The platoon of some twenty men responded well and was in good fighting form for our next firefight. We prepared well and were well prepared for any action.

Except the inaction of another leader.

I really don't know what happened, but a career sergeant had been assigned to the platoon. He was overweight and had not seen combat for who knows how long, if ever. I had little time to speak with him before we were airlifted and dropped into a landing zone for a mission.

I don't know how many days we humped the boonies, but I remember getting a call over the horn that we'd have an airdrop of supplies. It pissed me off when I saw them drop cans of soda. They were Fanta, a brand that I had never heard of and stayed away from for the rest of my life. Shortly after getting the drop, I stayed with one squad and moved far away from the drop area. I wanted no Viet Cong to zero in on us while we set up a makeshift camp in the jungle to spend the night.

I believe the sergeant took little preventative action. He simply stayed close to the site. And members of my platoon were wounded during a firefight that surprised them as they slept.

As you can expect, there was another investigation. They blamed the man in charge for those injured under fire.

They blamed me.

This time I felt different. This time I knew I was blameless. I had done everything by the book and then some. I fought with zeal and all my power to look out for the welfare of my men.

That's why I felt so much better when being relieved a second time. I knew I was a damn good leader. And members of my platoon agreed by organizing a mutiny when hearing that Lieutenant Colonel Salucci had fired me.

⋏   ⋏   ⋏

I had no idea what honor they had planned for me my last day on that hill in base camp. I really didn't expect anything and wonder whether there was some sort of mystical power guiding the troops to take their action in my favor. I focused all my attention on packing my few belongings—a camera I never got around to using and Plato's book, which I wanted to eventually reread. Getting all of my gear in order, I left my bunker and was walking off the hill when soldiers from the second squad called to me. They said they wanted to wish me well and to say goodbye.

We walked to the top of the firebase. I believe it was the highest point of the entire compound, and I saw other soldiers standing at attention, awaiting my arrival so that each could take part in loading the guns and firing them.

They fired them twenty-one times all total.

It was a twenty-one-gun salute!

I felt love and admiration mixed in with mutual respect and a growing sense of honor.

It was one of the few times in my life that I was speechless. Those sons of bitches went out of their way to pay their respects to me. They paid homage to a schmuck who had called mortar fire onto his own men. This mortar platoon honored me and provided me with something more lasting than any salute could have provided me then or now.

Forgiveness.

I didn't know how much of a gift they bestowed until years later, when reflecting on this event and when conditions were sufficient for this revelation to unfold.

I have no more reason to carry the guilt anymore. I am free. I always had been, but needed the time and the distance to finally see that.

The End

The object of war is not to die for your country but to make the other bastard die for his.

—US general George Patton

POSTSCRIPT: IT WAS ME THE VIET CONG WAS TRYING TO KILL

Someone was trying to kill me. Some motherfucker hiding in the trees, the bushes, the triple-canopy jungle had just shot at me and my platoon. I thought he was shooting randomly, despite the debris from the ground, grassland, and other tiny bits of rock that struck me from the bullet's ricochets.

He was aiming to kill me! It's taken me more than forty years to figure that out. Now I must try to answer the question of a lifetime: why I was spared and, more importantly, what I will do with the rest of this life after realizing I had been given a second chance to live it toward a much more pleasant ending.

Christ almighty! How could I not detect this attempt on my life in 1970? We had heard all the stories about the life expectancy of lieutenants—especially the second lieutenants, the lowest of what are called junior officers.

Who knows where that story originated? But there was some truth to it. The first person targeted by a good Vietnamese freedom fighter, aka the Viet Cong, was the leader but with only the single bar of a lieutenant designating his rank. Make the color of the bar a golden one—one we called a butter bar, for a second lieutenant—and everyone could see the sparkle as the lieutenant marched in his uniform. In the bush, however, all insignia on the uniforms were eventually darkened. I guess the top brass figured the enemy was smart enough to learn to read US Army ranking symbols. If you take out the leader of an army that outnumbers you, you create chaos, as the leaderless group can too easily flounder and forego its mission.

You shooting at me? I never knew till now!

I didn't bargain for this shit! Growing up in the city, I'd gotten into my share of fights, but no one ever shot at me. Some older fellows from Brewerytown in Philadelphia played with zip guns, handmade weapons that fired small .22-caliber bullets. They would shoot at each other in nearby Fairmount Park. But it was in fun, just like the game of Gestapo we'd play as we punched and tried to beat up opposing team members to get them to squeal or give up the secret password. We never hit them upside the head, only on the body and arms and legs. I never gave in but took the punches and ran away when I could.

But shooting me? Get the fuck out of here. My mama didn't raise no fool. I'd never have signed up for this job if I had known I'd become a marked man.

But there I was, the man in charge. Thank God for temporary stupidity. (It's kind of like temporary insanity, but that won't get you off in a court of law.) I never put the shooting together with the target of the shooter. I thought the sniper was simply pinning down the squad I was leading, not shooting directly at me, its leader.

I moved forward but fell back when another round of fire rang out in the distance. Again I felt some dirt and whatnot spray over me. But I still thought he was shooting at us as a group. Believe me, I never saw the enemy up close and only got glimpses of him from a distance as we'd approach one of his encampments.

I'd shoot in the direction of that glimpsed object, hoping I'd hit something or somebody. But I never knew whether I or someone else in my platoon had shot anyone unless we came across a body. That's the only time I ever came face to face with "Charlie," the nickname we gave the enemy.

No one engaged in hand-to-hand combat. We used no fixed bayonets, and I threw only two hand grenades the whole time I was in the field because we rarely got close enough to heave 'em. We'd have probably ended up hitting a branch and having the explosion backfire had I tossed any more.

Had I known then that an actual person was gunning for me, I think I would have acted differently. Wouldn't you? It would have shaken and instilled more fear in me. I'd have been more cautious and tentative in my actions and in following and passing on orders.

Oh, I'd have still gone a little berserk when someone got shot, and revenge would have sparked a fury that made one's actions foolishly heroic. I'd have charged like a madman when going to help a fallen soldier, as I did when learning that the Third Platoon had walked into an ambush and needed help from our platoon. To hell with my own safety. There were others worse off, and I believe I speak for every man I ever fought with by saying that any bravery we might have displayed arose from the love and compassion we had for the other guy.

ONE PUNCH DECKS CAPTAIN IN VIETNAM BASE CAMP FIGHT

But shit, man. This never happened to John Wayne. Rambo never got killed in any of his movies. We weren't supposed to die, and if we did, we'd go down swinging like Davy Crockett at the Alamo fighting through his last dying breath. At least, that's what every kid I grew up with believed after seeing his glory as depicted by Walt Disney fantasies and 1950s television.

Well, even if I had wanted to, there would have been nothing for me to do after realizing the Viet Cong was trying to kill me. I couldn't have just picked up and left South Vietnam. I had signed up for a two-year hitch with a nearly lifetime reserve clause when I accepted this officer's commission. What would have happened had I put down my rifle and tried to quit? I could have swung at my captain's jaw and sought some sort of security in the stockade, as did one of my troops on my very first day in a combat zone base camp.

"I'm not going into the field," this giant of a blond-haired Norwegian soldier told me as I walked in the base camp, introducing myself to platoon members resting between two-week patrols in the bush.

I advised him he'd be disciplined with an Article 15, an administrative punishment, or be placed in prison, aka the stockade.

"I don't care," he said, and that's what I reported to the captain when the commander asked me later how things went while meeting the troops.

The captain got pissed, left his bunk, and marched over to the bulky soldier. He ordered the private out of his sleeping quarters. Both were bare chested because of the extreme heat and relaxed decorum in the rear area.

They stood eye to eye as the thin, wiry captain threatened him with everything in the book.

Crunch!

I heard the sound echo off the commander's chin as the soldier answered with his fist, throwing a roundhouse at the captain's head and knocking him to the ground.

The man got demoted and ended up in the stockade, as I had said he would. I don't know whether that incident affected his discharge—that is, whether it was an honorable or dishonorable one. I never followed up with any of the men I met in Vietnam except for one, the third lieutenant in our company of one captain and three lieutenants. He found God outside Arkadelphia, Arkansas.

WHAT'S KEEPING THIS VET ALIVE ALL THESE YEARS?

I survived the war in Vietnam. Although I developed a slight hearing loss from artillery fire and claim it as a disability with the Veterans Administration, I was never physically wounded. But there are lots of psychological scars that flare up when stress triggers a traumatic memory. Despite this posttraumatic stress, I am pretty much intact.

Today, however, I have a question that only a much Higher Command can answer. Why was I spared? Why was another killed and not I? Is this just survivor guilt? I could have and perhaps should have been shot. But why was I not?

More importantly, what have I done with a life that was given me by fate or whatever power or source in the universe you want to name? What am I to do with myself now?

Whatever time I have left, dear Lord, just don't let me squander this second chance of mine. Just don't let me fuck up.

Let me tell my story, the one that I wanted to tell when I first came home from the war.

Let me get it right.

Let me tell of the fear and the heroics but also the damage done to the human psyche for the winners and the losers.

There are no winners in war. Why can't we make those who have never experienced a war understand that truth? Why can't we, the veterans of such wars, get that across to our families, to our neighborhoods, to our nations?

Maybe one lone voice crying in the wilderness could have an effect on that saber-rattling for yet another war.

ADDITIONAL READINGS

The following are articles I wrote about PTSD for my website, Contoveros. WordPress.Com.

Most were tough to write but helpful for something psychologists call "post-traumatic growth."

OWNING THE MENTAL ILLNESS AMONG US

https://contoveros.com/2015/12/09/
owning-the-mental-illness-amongst-us/

Mental illness scares the shit out of me. The very term conjures up images of some crazed guy with wild, straggly hair and a demon-like smile of malevolence. When I think of someone who might be a little touched in the head, a character Stephen King might write comes to mind.

I thought to myself, Who could ever admit to such a malady? You got to be crazy to be classified as one of the mentally ill.

And then one day it happened.

I admitted myself to an inpatient program after getting into three fights with assistant district attorneys in a courtroom in Philadelphia.

Yes, I became a little crazy. And now I'm admitting it to the world.

I got something psychologists and social workers now label as posttraumatic stress disorder. I kind of earned it in the Vietnam War. I found out later that more than 20 percent of Vietnam veterans have PTSD.

⋏　⋏　⋏

It wasn't always called PTSD. Prior to that, it was "battle fatigue" and "shell shock." Physicians at the time of the American Civil War called it "nostalgia." Among those exposed to military trauma, some reported missing home, feeling sad, sleep problems, and anxiety.

Another model of this condition included what some saw as a physical injury with typical symptoms. They called it "soldier's heart" or "irritable heart." Sufferers experienced a rapid pulse, anxiety, and trouble breathing. Soldiers were often returned to battle after receiving drugs to control symptoms. There were few if any studies conducted for veterans who returned home and suffered what we now call flashbacks.

I learned that the anger and rage that accompanies PTSD was actually written about thousands of years ago by a Greek poet named Homer when vocalizing the *Iliad.* Shakespeare mentioned it in his writings too!

▲   ▲   ▲

I got help for my malady at the Coatesville Medical Center, where I enrolled for what I thought was to be a two-week stint—a vacation of sorts, I believed. It turned out to be ten weeks with no time off for good behavior. I got a 100 percent disability rating out of it. Better still, I learned to meditate and keep the demons of my affliction in check through a daily practice.

I am proud to have sought the help and more importantly to be less intimidated to share it with all the crazy mother-humper types out there. You see, I believe we all have some kind of mental illness. Most of us hide it through our workload, drinking, or recreational drug consumption. But the brave ones seek counseling for the anger, the panic attacks, or that strange desire to vote for a Democrat in the next election.

Owning up to it and sharing it with another person is the first step in accepting what some might call the shadow side of ourselves. By bringing the shadow closer to the light, I believe we all can become enlightened.

PTSD ANGUISH SERVED UP AT BREAD STORE

https://contoveros.com/2009/11/26/
ptsd-anquish-served-up-at-bread-store/

Unappreciated. Unwanted. Unloved.

The child in me cries every time those emotions erupt. They come too often for me to ignore, and I finally meditated and traced my anger to its source and saw a truth: I felt unappreciated, unwanted, and unloved when the latest PTSD explosion occurred. And maybe now, after looking within and seeing how those feelings may have surfaced, I can cope with them better.

From what I learned, my mother nearly died giving birth to me. Baby Michael was shipped off to a farm in Mays Landing, New Jersey, where the grandmother raised the infant. The boy's father had been quoted as saying he would have preferred to see the son dead and not see the pain such a birth caused his wife.

Could any of this history have been absorbed by an infant? More importantly, could those long-suppressed feelings affect the baby-turned-man in middle age? Could they have contributed to events experienced in Vietnam that now mingle with the fears, anxieties, and sense of loss I feel?

That's my struggle with PTSD. I learn more about myself every day. Like today, I stopped at an outlet bread store for rolls. Picked up a dozen in a bag and walked to the counter. An older man was standing there, waiting for an order he'd made the day before. The young man behind the counter appeared rushed. It was before noon on the day before Thanksgiving, and the store was already crowded.

I placed my bag on the empty counter, hoping that I could quickly pay and get out to complete some other chore. But the young man did not look at me. He simply said "Wait a second" when I moved my bag closer to his line of vision. No luck in getting quick service here.

The clerk left the counter. Returned and said something under his breath, only to leave the sales area a second time for the bakery in back. Other customers had walked up behind me with multiple bags of breads, rolls, pies, and whatnot.

When the clerk returned, he laid two big boxes on the counter. I had to remove my bag and place it beside the cash register. The older man paid for his goods and had trouble getting them out of the door some eight feet away.

"Here, let me help you," I said, opening and holding the door for him to get by. I felt good to have provided him service. But when I returned to the register, the couple that was behind me was now being waited upon. Their order seemed to go on and on.

My patience, however, did not!

"A good deed never goes unpunished," I said, loud enough for the cashier to hear me. Either he did not or, worse, he ignored me. The woman in line, however, did hear and offered an apology.

"I'm not mad at you," I said to her and the man accompanying her. "I'm mad at this asshole!" My anger rose as I still was unable to get the son of a bitch cashier's attention. He continued to look at the register, ignoring my challenge to his lack of courtesy.

As the man and woman looked at me, I knew I had done wrong.

"I'm sorry," I said, adding, "I have PTSD," as if that could explain my rude behavior. I threw the bag of rolls to the floor and walked out of the store, blowing all other chores I had intended to complete.

"God, why am I hyperalert and hypersensitive?" I asked. "Please make me calm, mellow. Just don't make death the only way for me to find that peace."

EXPRESSWAY HEART
LEADS TO EQUANIMITY

https://contoveros.com/2017/05/24/
expressway-of-a-heart-leads-to-equanimity/amp/

I wanted the driver who cut me off to crash and burn.

For a brief moment, I thought of praying that he would immediately die for cutting in front of me as I was doing sixty miles an hour on the expressway behind a car just five lengths in front of me. I beeped my horn and flashed my high beams at the driver. I relished the hatred I felt burning inside of me. I loathed him from the bottom of my heart and wanted a bloody accident to befall him.

Oh my god. What are you doing, Michael J.? You want peace and calm in your world but only when it's convenient to you, when you're alone or with like-minded people. Once you face the hustle and the bustle of people with little concern for you, you become that son of a bitch you claim you're so far above because of the loving compassion you want to provide others. You're a hypocrite when the rubber actually hits the road, for, during those stressful moments, you still blame your response on PTSD.

Those moments occur more and more frequently on the road since you retired. It is on an expressway of life that you face your most stressful entanglements nowadays.

⋏ ⋏ ⋏

Remember two days earlier, when you experienced a flashback to the Vietnam War? You were driving to Center City, Philadelphia, and felt you were in a firefight. Your heart sped up, your breathing increased rapidly, and your hands were sweating as you maneuvered through the traffic on the Schuylkill Expressway. You barely escaped injury by steering to the far lane of the four-lane highway and found an opening for several hundred feet as you sped up, weaving from lane to lane. You were rushing to a spiritual gathering, one you had been late for a week earlier, and you didn't want to be shamefully late again.

You wanted to stop all traffic at that moment. All of life. You wanted to bring to an end all involvement outside of your home, outside of your safe and secure cave. You wanted to withdraw and have nothing to do with anything outside of that safe and secure womb.

And then it dawned on you. All you wanted was happiness and for all others to be happy as you recalled the prayer learned from one of the Buddhist teachings.

"May all beings have happiness and the cause of happiness.
May they be free of suffering and the cause of suffering.
May they never be separated from the happiness which knows no suffering.
May they live in equanimity, free from attachment and aversion."

The motorist was not free from attachments. You were not free from aversions. You both wanted the same thing in life, but neither one quite knew how to obtain it.

You immediately forgave the driver. Who knows what was going through the person's mind or what suffering they felt? We've all been in similar situations, rushing for some all-important meeting or to avoid some illusory, mind-created catastrophe.

You then forgave yourself and felt the heat of anger begin to dissipate on the road.

Here's hoping that you can repeat this exercise the next time you travel this way.

QUIXOTE BATTLES PTSD
IN PHILLY COURT

https://contoveros.com/2010/06/26/
don-quixote-battles-ptsd-in-philly-courts/

I never felt more like Don Quixote than when I represented a woman charged with a crime.

And while I didn't want to become a champion just for women defendants, I'd felt called to champion her, even when it cost me my reputation, my sanity, and my very career as a trial attorney.

I provided dignity to clients as a public defender, especially the women. Heroin addicts became respected ladies who needed someone to tell their story to a court system most of them were unaccustomed to battling. Many with only a minimum education became learned seers who knew more of surviving in the world than many with MAs and PhDs.

I took up the sword and fought like there was no tomorrow. Two women, both white, come to my mind. Both got lured by heavy drugs. One faced a mandatory sentence for purchasing a gun for a drug supplier who just happened to be a felon. She had cervical cancer and simply wanted to be with her family and child during treatment instead of receiving it while at the women's facility of the state prison in Muncy, Pennsylvania.

The other woman, also a heroin user, was out on the streets, having just gotten high with her boyfriend when she put the needle into a rumpled jacket for later use and went to a Rite Aid drugstore to get deodorant and other sundry goods.

She stuffed them into her jacket pocket, the one holding the needle, with plans to walk out without paying. In other words, be a shoplifter. She'd done it before. At the same Rite Aid.

Someone at the store recognized her, she told me when I visited her in a local Philadelphia prison several months after her arrest. Yes, Virginia, there really is incarceration for people with criminal records, despite what others want you to believe. She sat in jail some four months before her case was called to trial. I requested a continuance for further corroboration of her story.

See, two men stopped her in the store. A manager grabbed her from the rear, and a clerk got to her up front. She tried to leave and resisted as they held her. She claimed one held her by her hair. The other pulled the stolen items from her jacket pocket.

She clutched the needle as it spilled from her jacket and cut her hand, she told me, showing a slight scar on her finger. One of the men saw the needle and claimed she twisted it and positioned it so that she could stab 'em with it. She never did. One man testified that she actually swung her arm in an attempt, he wanted the court to believe, to possibly inject them with a taointed needle, according to an assistant district attorney (ADA).

After the young woman was placed in prison, a test showed she had hepatitis B.

⋏　⋏　⋏

A specially assigned ADA was appointed to prosecute her with an initial charge of attempted murder.

"It was a false positive," the woman told me of the test. She claimed she had proof from some doctor that she wasn't contagious. I use the word "contagious" for lack of a better medical understanding. I immediately started an investigation to confirm this information to share it with the ADA, a woman I had worked with before and respected.

The case came to court, and I advised the young prosecutor of the woman's claim to show a lack of intent to cause such grave injury. I went into detail, sharing my information in hopes of securing a plea for a lesser offense than aggravated assault, which would have required my client serve a minimum of five years in jail, mainly because of her record. It was a long one made up of drug possession cases and lots of shoplifting.

"When did she learn it was a false positive?" the prosecutor asked, refusing to lower an offer of five to ten years. I started to tell her, and she let slip her reason for the question. Had my client not known it was a false positive until after having been arrested and sent to jail, then the ADA could prove *intent* at the time of the shoplifting incident.

I went ballistic. Flashed back to Vietnam. Suffered perhaps the worst episode of PTSD that has ever surfaced in my life.

I reverted to the first lieutenant who realized a member of his platoon was placed in immediate danger. By me. In my efforts to help, I made it worse.

"Get out of here!" I yelled to the ADA while huddled at the bar of the court. "Get the fuck out of here!" I added through a clenched jaw while pointing to a door leading out of the courtroom. A sheriff had just brought the defendant into the Philadelphia Criminal Justice Center courtroom, and I felt justified in demanding the prosecutor leave so I could maintain confidentiality with my client at the defense table in the open court.

⚔ ⚔ ⚔

Several lawyers, defendants, and witnesses with other cases, as well as police, sat stunned as they watched my over-the-top behavior. I didn't care. Instead I played to them all, pointing out that in my opinion, the ADA (who was straight out of what's called the "Habitual Offender Unit") was trying to get a conviction for the worst offense instead of seeking justice.

I stopped practicing law about a month later. Got into a few more blowups with prosecutors while awaiting treatment for PTSD and clearing my schedule of trial work for a month. That's the amount of time I thought I would need to cure myself.

It's been two years this month since I left. Not sure what happened to either woman. Other lawyers were appointed to champion their causes. Today I liken old myself to a Don Quixote with a foolish hope to right all wrongs and tilt at windmills. After all, "they might be giants!" I like what I see in the mirror now and, more importantly, the dreamer still within me.

Here's to you, my Dulcinea!

DAMN WAR TO HELL AND TAKE PTSD WITH IT

https://contoveros.com/2010/02/03/damn-war-to-hell-take-ptsd-with-it/

D amn PTSD.

Here I am, trying to gain composure, sitting in a car parked in a lot at Lee's, a produce mart outside Conshohocken, Pennsylvania. Don't know how many customers have come and gone seeing this middle-aged man with eyes closed, silently breathing, trying to erase what he did just a few short moments ago. Actually, some ten minutes have passed since I collapsed from the latest spike of uncontrolled adrenalin.

I feel I just went a little mad. Shot out of a weapon like a bullet. Wanting to strike the nearest enemy, to do harm, to hurt someone for hurting me. I had driven recklessly, tailgating a guy who did not slow as I tried to merge into traffic as I was leaving a CVS pharmacy. He sped up. I could have just eaten that slight done to me. Brush it off as just an inconsiderate gesture done in an inconsiderate world. But I have stressed out already, and I made a federal case out of his bad behavior by making mine worse.

The posttraumatic stress disorder, aka PTSD, kicked in. I gunned the engine and raced my car to catch up to his vehicle, coming dangerously close to his rear. He was no dummy. He applied his brakes to scare me off. I do it when someone is tailing too close to me. But I didn't bite: I sped up and screeched to a halt at the last possible moment, causing heads to turn among pedestrians as well as those in cars at my side and to the rear. It shook him. But not completely.

Both cars started again immediately after the near collision. I tried to see the guy, make out his features, but couldn't. Must have been in his twenties, no more than twenty-five. I just want to teach him a lesson about the rules of the road.

There's daylight in the passing lane. Now I'll slip by him...

And cut in front of him...not knowing what he may do next, because I cannot look at him...I have to keep all of my attention on this frenzied driving. Now I cut in front of the next car, but not as abruptly. He didn't do anything to me. But here I am endangering everybody...

My God, what am I doing? Who the hell am I? What have I become?

I have to get away; must pull over. But not here, a little further up the road. Lee's Fresh Produce. Pull your car into the store's lot, Michael. Seek refuge. Seek help.

But there is none, really, is there? You'll have this sickness for the rest of your life. You should not drive. Should not deal with stress. Should be put away for your own protection...to protect everybody closest to you so that you won't try to hurt anyone again. Should not have lived to come home from Vietnam. There, you finally said it. Again.

⋏　⋏　⋏

Therapy the next day helps. My psychologist, Dr. Howard Cohen, says there's been an improvement. That I saw the hole I had dug and jumped in but was able to get out and look back to know exactly what the "it" was: PTSD. Some veterans believe it is themselves causing this bizarre behavior. That the rage they now feel is just part of their makeup. That they're made this way, and that nothing can help them. They're wrong, and I hope we can help them. Acknowledging that there is a problem is generally a good first step.

Damn the war. Damn the military. Damn the PTSD.

Please, my United States of America, stop all the fighting before the fighting stops all of us.

OMEGA OPENS DOOR TO LOST PTSD VETERANS

https://contoveros.com/2012/04/23/
omega-opens-doors-to-lost-pts-veterans/

I didn't want to go back to Omega Institute this year. Each time I traveled to this land of Sleepy Hollow and Rip Van Winkle, I'd get high from the holistic experience. But then I'd change into an Ichabod Crane, feeling chased by the Headless Horseman, who'd tell true life stories that caused so much pain I couldn't hold it inside.

Two years ago I picked up a chair and slammed it to the floor after being unable to console an Iraqi veteran, a colonel who was close to my age, who spoke of losing the one and only love of his entire life. He was willing to convert and become a Muslim until his wonderful Iraqi translator fiancée was killed by the very people we had been sent to win over for democracy. I wanted to cry out, to sob, but instead the rage in me poured out.

Last year I stormed out of a small group session when a similar situation occurred. I couldn't tolerate these group sessions where you were required to listen deeply but offer no compassion or understanding to someone who had just opened their veins to you. I wanted (and needed) to respond in some way to show that I felt their pain, their suffering. I wanted to take on that pain and suffering, even for just a little while, to help reduce it.

And so I discarded the letter from Omega advising me of the seminar called "Real Cost of War" with Claude "AnShin" Thomas, the Vietnam veteran and helicopter machine gunner who later became a Zen Buddhist monk to help others like him with posttraumatic stress disorder. I know I caused a ruckus when I lost control and took it out on the metal chair. I don't know why I did it. I hardly ever slam or break things when a PTS episode erupts. Despite my efforts to meditate and develop loving-kindness and compassion, I now know I have this thread of PTSD that has gotten all jumbled up with other parts that make up the whole of me. I can't remove it without unraveling everything else, so I will have it until the day I die. I want to recognize it, keep it in check, and, more importantly, be able to forgive myself for the crazy things I do when the rage arises unchecked inside of me.

⋏　⋏　⋏

Like the time I went shopping at a PetSmart near my Conshohocken, Pennsylvania, home. While driving in the parking lot, I noticed that some-one in a shiny new white van had taken up two parking spots.

"Damn it," I said, slowly passing the vehicle, looking for another place to park. I stopped immediately on seeing the driver of the van get out of the vehicle and walk toward the store.

"Excuse me," I called out to him. "You took up two spaces there." I tried to point out the mistake he must have surely overlooked making.

He looked in my direction and said something but continued to walk to the entrance door.

"Yo, man, you're taking up two spaces," I said, my voice rising along with a growing feeling of a manifest injustice.

He never looked back but went into the store.

"Hey, you!" I shouted by this time, letting venom spew out with a choice follow-up: "You motherfucker."

I gunned the car engine and quickly pulled into an open parking spot further away.

Rushing into the store, I tried to find him. All of the men began to look alike, and after stopping two fellows who had no idea about some white-van parking violation I had quizzed them on, I got my supplies and went to the cashier.

I started to calm down and come to my senses but ended up telling the cashier about the double–parking space scoundrel. It was the worst thing I could have done. She understood my feelings all right but then told me how much she hated persons without handicap plates parking in a handicap spot, like the one she needed to use at her apartment complex.

"I'd call the police, but they wouldn't show up for the longest time, and the guy would be gone by then," she said. Leaning forward and speaking in a conspiratorial tone, she confided that one time she got so mad she keyed a car illegally parked in a handicap spot.

"What do you mean by keying?" I asked.

She motioned with her hand as if holding a key between her fingers while sliding the metal device all across the side of the car.

I got shocked hearing this from such a peaceful-looking grandmother type. God, talk about violence, I thought. At that precise moment, just as she was ringing up my order but before I could pay for it, I saw the white van driver exiting the store.

"Hey, man!" I yelled, telling the cashier that I'd be right back. I rushed toward the guy, trying to get his attention. He wouldn't look back as I made it to the door and saw him getting into his vehicle.

I screamed louder and went toward the van as he started the engine and began to back up. *Motherfucker*s got mixed in with some *cocksucker*s (think rooster strutting here!) as I pushed the envelope of my behavior, which should have pissed off any reasonable person and made them stop. He didn't. So I did what any other Vietnam veteran with PTS would have done—I kicked the door of his shiny new white van.

That did the trick. He stopped driving, got out of the van, and stood in the street, looking down from his six-foot, three-inch frame to my five-six height (on my tallest days).

He got in my face, but I didn't back away. At least one fellow, a bystander who saw the incident, tried to break up what had the makings of a real street brawl.

"Why did you take up two spots?" I yelled up at him, still trying to take the moral high ground in a world my PTS tells me is often lacking such moral justice. When he didn't answer, I yelled again and then threw in the worst epitaph any man living would hate to be given upon his death: "You fuckin' pussy."

Now, those are fighting words where I come from, and I don't know why I said them. Furthermore, I couldn't figure out why he tried to insult me back by calling me a "fat fucker."

Again, I shouted the f- and p-words at him. I didn't care what he might do, because I felt like an avenging angel riding a wave of righteous indignation. I also knew that I could get him for assault if he laid a finger on me, despite any damage my foot might have caused when I kicked the van. I had practiced criminal law for twenty years before PTSD finally interrupted my peaceful and loving relationship as a public defender with some of Philly's worst criminals. I knew from personal knowledge that causing property damage gives no one the right to physically assault another, particularly when the person had crossed the line of societal parking etiquette and rules. He had to learn people weren't going to take this anymore, particularly people like us crazed-Vietnam-vet types who get fueled by a weird sense of moral outrage at something as minor as a parking incident.

Come to think of it, most, if not all, of my PTSD episodes involve simple things where I end up making mountains out of molehills. I go from zero to sixty in the flash of a millisecond. It was great to use such a technique in combat, but it could be deadly to me when used at home.

Luckily, this incident broke up before escalating any further. A young fellow walking past interrupted us, and it was enough for us to break up the encounter. It stuck with me, and whenever I see an injustice taking place, I have to be very careful with my actions.

⋏　⋏　⋏

I have no idea what lesson I was supposed to learn or what action I was supposed to take from this moment of karma arising. Worse yet, I had no one I could talk to who might understand the craziness I dealt with week to week. I never knew when something might trigger an explosion.

"Why do I even let myself out to mingle with reasonable people," I thought, "when I should be locked up for my safety and the good of others? I'm afraid for myself and more so for others. At times I feel completely lost."

That's when I began to rethink the Omega Institute experience, and I remembered how good I felt being around people like myself, veterans who weren't ashamed (or afraid anymore) of talking about PTS. I included among them the family members of vets who suffer not only from the vet's actions but also from what medical folks call secondary PTS.

The yearning to see them again, to hear their stories and to tell them of my homeland battles, kicked in, and I recovered the Omega letter, contacted the institute, and lucked out with a scholarship. I figured I'd use something called "noble speech" to get around the maintain-silence-at-all-costs rule and discuss mutual problems while gaining some insights there.

Everything seemed to be going well until Thursday morning, when I saw the black-robed, bald-headed monk walk in the crowded hall of the Lake Theatre of Omega. I went to greet him, seeing him for the first time with a cane, and I jokingly asked if I should provide him with a full prostration at his feet like I did on a previous occasion, and he said, "Just don't go slamming any more chairs to the floor."

Despite the words, I felt lots of love and compassion as he smiled, and I knew no chair would come between me and this helicopter-crew-chief guru, Claude AnShin Thomas.

I felt I was at home again. I felt I was where I belonged, PTS or no PTS.

PTSD RAISES MONSTER HEAD FROM TOILET

https://contoveros.com/2009/11/14/
ptsd-raises-its-monster-head-from-toilet/)

Put a straitjacket on me.
Hide me in a padded room.
Get me away from people. All people who I can harm with my PTSD.
I had another one of those days. The ones that end up with my saying I'm sorry over and over for something stupid I did. Something in which I make a mountain out of a molehill. Why do I believe such events pose life and death to me? Why can't I react like a normal person, perhaps get a little angry but not lash out with a cry in my voice and the feeling that I am facing certain doom?

⚓   ⚓   ⚓

It all started in the morning. Going to the bathroom. (It should never happen this early in the day, but it often it explodes at the crack of dawn.)

My son had deposited another one of his incredibly hard stools in the basin of the toilet. A plunger stuck out from the toilet. I should have taken a clue right then. Someone had tried to perform an emergency plumbing operation and must have left without success.

Well, I'm the best plumber in this house, I thought. They don't know how to plunge. They give up too soon.

And there I pushed. And pushed. To no avail.

The water rose to the top of the porcelain edge and ever so slowly began pouring out of the bowl of the toilet onto the floor below.

"Jesus Christ!" I hollered, waking everyone in the household. "We're going to have to call a plumber."

I backed up from the toilet, waiting for the water to recede. It must recede, I prayed. It did, so I plunged away. And once again the water rose, flowing more quickly now, and soon it joined the existing puddle, forcing its mass of liquid from the small bathroom floor to the carpeted hallway outside.

I threw towels and bathmats on the floor, trying my best to stem the tide. When I got it under control, I turned to the important business of the day: getting fully awake to get my son out of the house and off to school before seven o'clock.

▲   ▲   ▲

I stood before the bathroom mirror. Had to lean in, for I wore no glasses. They'd broken weeks ago, and I'd had to wear contact lenses. Do you know how tough it is to go fourteen to eighteen hours with contacts covering your pupils? Well, I reached for the lens case, put in the right lens, and then tackled the more difficult left side.

The lens disappeared! I looked on my fingers, my hand, and my arm. No lens. I moved my eyelid up and down, back and forth, eventually rubbing my left eye as hard as possible to feel whether the lens had somehow got stuck there.

Next, I surrendered to panic.

"Nicholas!" I hollered, but not as loudly as when I had spoken the Lord's name earlier. "I need your help!"

My son was fully dressed when he entered the small room. With the eye of an eagle, he spotted the lens on the floor that I had just mopped with clean, fluffy towels.

"Go ahead and brush," I advised him. "No, not that brush," I yelled, almost as loudly as I had when calling on Jesus. "That's mine. Have you been using my toothbrush?!"

Not to be outdone by my yelling, Nicholas hollered that it was his toothbrush and that he had been using it for days. But it was the only gray brush on the vanity, and I'd only opened its packaging some three days earlier.

I gave in, told him to keep the brush, and grabbed the old one I had replaced but not thrown out. I was going to use that for cleaning grout. I replaced it because I found that brush had been moved from my regular spot, and I figured someone else used it to clean their grubby little teeth.

▲   ▲   ▲

The contact lens rebelled. It refused to stay in the eye. It hurt every time I laid it on the surface of the eyeball, and after the fifth or sixth time, I wanted to fall down crying in full view of my son. No one should have to endure the toilet challenge plus the lens battle within a few measly minutes of each other on the same morning.

"Brush!" I hollered, seeing that my son was waiting for me to move back from the mirror. "You're going to be late!"

"No one can talk to me like that!" he yelled just as loudly, then stepped to the door, about to slam it, when I rushed out, pushing him back him into the bathroom and giving him the privacy that he should have been given earlier.

Patiently (sort of) waiting outside, I heard my wife yell at me not to yell at our son.

"You don't know what I have just gone through!" spilled out of me, as if that were going to explain my tantrum and somehow ease the tension that was getting more and more palpable in our household. Not sure who said what next or who told the other to go to hell, but I stormed into the bathroom as soon as Nicholas finished, and I finally got the lens in place.

I also apologized to my son, who was gracious enough to say nothing. My wife, though, did not accept my mea culpa.

"You're always sorry," she correctly observed, causing me to react with another choice word or two before leaving the bedroom.

▲   ▲   ▲

Finally downstairs, I saw Nicholas off to school, feeling as low as the temperature had dipped the night before. I am sick, I thought. I am no good.

I glanced toward the floor. My cat, Sundance, looked up at me. I felt a slight smile come over me. She's my "Buddha Buddy," you see: she sits on my lap when I meditate. And so she did this morning, following me to a seat, then jumping up and snuggling into place for our joint relaxation excursion.

Twenty minutes or more went by. I felt refreshed. Revived. Forgiven. I thought of the straightjacket and the padded walls and how much of a monster PTSD has created inside of me. But there also exists a kind, friendly small child inside, and he calmed down the one lacking impulse control.

When I returned upstairs, the toilet somehow worked properly again. The sun was shining, and I looked forward to a new day.

"POSTTRAUMATIC GROWTH" HELPS YOU HEAL

https://contoveros.com/2015/12/30/
posttraumatic-growth-can-help-you-heal/

I have experienced something scientists have labeled "posttraumatic growth" twice in my life and some fifty years apart. Both led to major changes in my life and a new look at life that I'd never imagined was possible.

Being freshly discharged from the US Army following a stint in Vietnam, I enrolled in a community college and studied like there was no tomorrow. You see, I had left my so-called academic career at Bishop Neumann High School in South Philadelphia when I got caught playing hooky, and preferring not go to summer school for religion, I opted to get a technical education for the art and craft of printing. I had no college experience when I was commissioned an officer, and I knew nothing about higher education except for the doofuses I met among the officer corps who had little or no street smarts.

I studied journalism, and I excelled. I spent more than forty hours a week studying, often taking more than the required number of credits to be a full-time student and get a whopping $525 a month from the GI Bill. Twice I took twenty-one credits in one semester and held a GPA placing me on the dean's list.

What does PTSD have to do with it?

I felt that I'd failed in the Vietnam War. I had failed my men who got injured; I had failed my brother, who guided me through Officer Candidate School; and I had failed myself and the expectations I raised for being a soldier.

I would not fail this time, I said to myself, becoming editor of my college newspaper while winning a Sigma Delta Chi scholarship for journalism and a fellowship to study state government in Pennsylvania's capital city, Harrisburg.

I then got a bachelor of arts degree in one year and then a master of arts degree one year later, completing in four years what it normally took others six years to complete. I was determined to overcome the trauma of the war. And I found I could do it while having fun.

⚔ ⚔ ⚔

Now fast-forward to 2008, when I failed at being a caregiver for my wife, who had suffered a traumatic brain injury two years earlier. Wendy Wright Contos was a copy editor at the *Philadelphia Inquirer* and fell down the steps in our Conshohocken, Pennsylvania, home. I took care of her for two straight years, but then I suffered caregiver burnout. I also had to deal with PTSD from the war and the ever-growing stress from representing poor defendants in the criminal justice system of Philadelphia. I had to eventually place my wife in an assisted living facility, and she passed away some three years ago.

This perfect storm of emotional and mental trauma, however, forced me to seek help, stop working, and find guidance from different spiritual paths. I lucked out because of my trauma from the war. I got paid by the Veterans Administration to look after my wife and get my teenage son through high school without committing myself to an inpatient clinic for help.

I found strength and guidance after dealing with the trauma, and it has made me into the man I am today.

Writing a blog, starting in 2009, under my father's name of Contoveros helped greatly. I am still flawed but more confident that I am walking a path I was destined to seek, despite the sufferings. I believe I now understand posttraumatic growth!

The Posttraumatic Stress Growth Inventory:
  Appreciation of life
  Relationships with others
  New possibilities in life
  Personal strength
  Spiritual change

SONGS

"Universal Soldier" is a song written and recorded by Canadian singer-songwriter Buffy Sainte-Marie in 1964 and made popular by Donavan in 1965.

"Abraham, Martin and John" is a 1968 song written by Dick Holler and first recorded by Dion.

"I-Feel-Like-I'm-Fixin'-to-Die Rag" by Country Joe and the Fish, 1965

"Hey Jude" is a song by the Beatles, written by Paul McCartney, August 1968.

"Leaving on a Jet Plane" is a song written by John Denver in 1966 and most famously recorded by Peter, Paul and Mary.

"We Gotta Get out of This Place," The Animals, 1965

"Still in Saigon" by the Charlie Daniels Band (1982) and written by songwriter Dan Daley in 1981.

BOOKS AND OTHER WRITINGS

Hanh, Thich Nhat. *Love in Action: Writings on Nonviolent Social Change*. With a foreword by Daniel Berrigan. Berkeley, California: Parallax, 1993.

The Sixties Project. Sponsored by Viet Nam Generation and the Institute of Advanced Technology in the Humanities at the University of Virginia at Charlottesville.

BOOKS BY CONTOVEROS, AKA MICHAEL J. CONTOS

Francis of Assisi, a Novel Awakening to Lady Poverty. Under the pseudonym Francesco diBernadone. CreateSpace, 2014.

Mystical Insights, My Odyssey to Ithaca. Under the name of Contoveros. CreateSpace, 2015.

A Brewerytown Kid Grows Up. Under birth name, Michael J. Contos. CreateSpace, 2017.

Made in the USA
Middletown, DE
07 September 2021

47741439R00146